RURAL INDUSTRIES

OF THE LUNE VALLEY

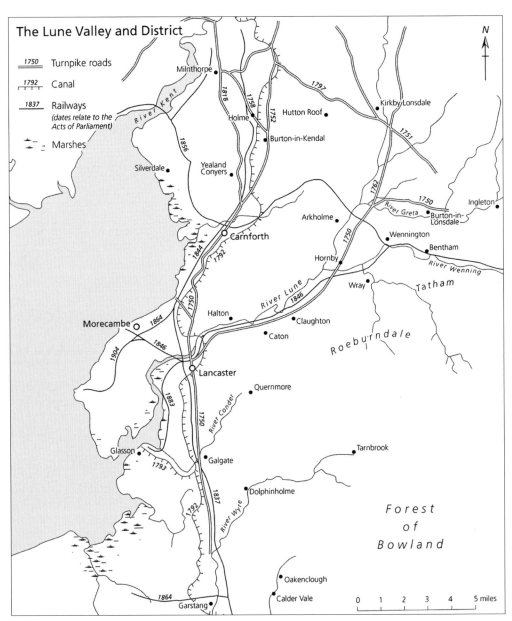

The Lune Valley and District

_1750_ Turnpike roads

_1792_ Canal

_1837_ Railways
(dates relate to the
Acts of Parliament)

Marshes

N

Milnthorpe
1797
Kirkby Lonsdale
River Kent
1818
1758
1752
Holme
Hutton Roof
1856
Burton-in-Kendal
1751
Silverdale
Yealand Conyers
1762
1750
Ingleton
Arkholme
River Greta
Burton-in-Lonsdale
1844
1792
Carnforth
Wennington
1750
Bentham
Hornby
River Wenning
1750
Wray
Tatham
River Lune
1846
Morecambe
1864
Halton
Claughton
1904
1846
Caton
Roeburndale
Lancaster
1883
1750
Quernmore
River Conder
Glasson
1793
Galgate
Tarnbrook
1792
1837
Dolphinholme
River Wyre
Forest
of
Bowland
Oakenclough
1864
Calder Vale
Garstang

0 1 2 3 4 5 miles

Map drawn by Chris Beacock.

Rural Industries
of the Lune Valley

Editor: Michael Winstanley

Centre for North-West Regional Studies
University of Lancaster
2000

Rural Industries of the Lune Valley

This volume is the 43rd in a series published by the Centre for North-West Regional Studies at the University of Lancaster

Text copyright © Michael Winstanley, Barbara Pidcock, Phil Hudson, Emmeline Garnett, Christine Workman, James Price, 2000

Published by the Centre for North-West Regional Studies, University of Lancaster

Designed and typeset by Carnegie Publishing Ltd, Carnegie House, Chatsworth Road, Lancaster LA1 4SL

Printed and bound in the UK by The Cromwell Press, Trowbridge

British Library Cataloguing-in-Publication Data
A CIP catalogue record for this book is available from the British Library

ISBN 1–86220-094-7

Contents

Preface

This book has been a long time in the making. It was originally conceived back in 1996 when Elizabeth Roberts, then Director of the Centre for North-West Regional Studies, approached the contributors who were then all actively engaged in their individual research projects. The current editor took over when Elizabeth retired in 1999. Since then new information has continued to come to light which has necessitated further amendments to contributions already submitted. In addition to the individual acknowledgements in each chapter and captions for illustrations, the editor would like to thank Jean Turnbull, the new administrator of the Centre, Lancaster City Museums for their generous assistance with photographs, Chris Beacock for cartographic services, and all the contributors for their patience and forebearance in answering the editor's numerous queries.

Researching the past is like doing a jigsaw without knowing what the final picture will look like and knowing all along that some, often many, of the pieces will be missing, lost forever to posterity. The pictures presented in this book are as complete as the authors have been able to make them in the time, and space, available. Should any readers know of other pieces in the jigsaws, however, the contributors would be happy to hear from them care of the Centre for North-West Regional Studies. The joy of the past is that there is always more to learn about it.

Michael Winstanley
History Department
Lancaster University

March 2000

Abbreviations

LRO   Lancashire Record Office (Preston)
PRO   Public Record Office (Kew)
OS   Ordnance Survey
GSD   George Smith's Diaries
HSLC   *Historic Society of Lancashire and Cheshire*
PP   Parliamentary Papers
TLCAS   *Transactions of the Lancashire and Cheshire Antiquarian Society*
TCWAAS   *Transactions of the Cumberland & Westmorland Antiquarian and Archaeological Society*

Notes on contributors

Emmeline Garnett is a retired schoolteacher with a degree in English but a passion for local and family history. Among her many interests are the dated buildings of South Lonsdale and Bentham, and the history of the Hornby Castle estate.

Phil Hudson runs 'Hudson History' in Settle, where he writes, sells and publishes local history books and journals, including *Yorkshire History Quarterly* and *Lancashire History Quarterly*.

Barbara Pidcock has been a practising hand-loom weaver for more than 25 years, exhibiting and selling in Sussex, Lancashire and Cumbria. After taking the Local History Diploma at Lancaster University (1989–91) she now combines the practical with the historical.

James Price is Head of Geography at St Martin's College, Lancaster. His interest in, and publications on, the industrial archaeology and architectural history of Lancaster and its hinterland date back over many years.

Michael Winstanley is Senior Lecturer in History at Lancaster University. He researches the regional history of the North West during the nineteenth century, with a particular focus on the social and economic development of the Lancaster area.

Christine Workman is a History teacher at Lancaster Girls' Grammar School who, since taking the Local History Diploma at Lancaster University in 1989, has researched a variety of aspects of the Lune Valley's history.

CHAPTER ONE

Lunesdale and the Industrial Revolution

Michael Winstanley

Extolled by topographers, travel guides, poets and artists alike since the late eighteenth century as the 'perfect landscape of the extensive sort', the Lune Valley has generally been portrayed since as a tranquil, rural retreat apparently untouched by the ravages of industrialisation. J. M. W. Turner's famous painting from above Crook of Lune at Caton has increasingly come to symbolise this vision. Yet appearances and reputations can be deceptive. The prominent character in the foreground of Turner's panorama is not a bucolic rustic, but a workman wielding a pickaxe, and evidence of extensive quarrying and coal mining from this time can still be found throughout the district. The valley was also riding on the crest of an industrial wave when the artist passed through it in 1816. All the major settlements along the Lune and its tributaries – Caton, Halton, Hornby, Wray, Bentham, Ingleton, Burton in Lonsdale, Kirkby Lonsdale and Sedbergh – boasted either textile mills engaged in spinning a variety of materials – silk, cotton, worsted, woollens and flax – or significant numbers of weavers. Villages to the north and south of Lancaster such as Holme, Galgate, Dolphinholme and Scorton were also booming and there were even mills in small isolated settlements at Westhouse, Leck, Lee and Catshaw in Wyresdale. Wray, and nearby Quernmore and Over Wyresdale, had significant colonies of hat manufacturers. Burton in Lonsdale was a centre of pottery production. Basket-making was firmly established in Arkholme.

The studies in this book are about some of the district's lost industries and their contribution to its development.[1] This introduction seeks to set them within the wider context of the economic development of Britain, primarily from the mid-eighteenth century, and to discuss their significance for the people who worked in them.

Industrial expansion

By the early nineteenth century, most settlements of any size in the valley depended not just on agriculture but on the employment opportunities generated by mining, quarrying and manufacturing. With the exception of basket-making and possibly pottery, these local industries did not conform to the image of 'traditional' rural handicraft trades which have been so admired by an urban public since the late nineteenth-century and promoted by the Arts and Crafts Movement and numerous official and voluntary organisations ever since. They were also relatively recent arrivals, manifestations of broader changes in the British economy. Indeed, there is little evidence of any substantial industrial activity before the second half of the eighteenth century. As Barbara Pidcock's chapter shows, domestic textile production in the Lune Valley in the early modern period was negligible in comparison to that in south-east Lancashire, and a similar study of North Craven has also uncovered very little activity.[2] References to flax dressers began to appear in the valley from the early eighteenth century, but most cloth production still remained confined to towns along the coast.[3] Coal mining and stone quarrying had long been widespread, but they were characterised by small-scale, low-key and intermittent concerns. A detailed survey of the Hornby Estate in 1751 reveals that rental from its slate quarries was only £5 per annum and that customary and free tenants had access to them for their own uses. The right to mine Tatham coals was let for just £12, but the pits and those at Farleton were considered to be 'quite worn out'. 'Several trials' had concluded that 'there is no other Coal on Hornby Estate'. Lead prospecting at Botton Head was under way at the time but this also proved fruitless.[4] Commercial pottery production at Burton can only be dated back to the 1740s and 1750s.[5] Basket-makers began to appear in parish registers in the late eighteenth century. The number of hatters in Lancaster's freeman rolls doubled in the second half of the century during which time there were also significant increases in Quernmore and Over Wyresdale. Virtually every textile mill in the area was established between the end of the American War of Independence in 1783 and the mid-1790s, somewhat earlier than nearby Lancaster, where, with the exception of a small mill at White Cross in 1802, there was no substantial capital investment in factories until steam was more widely adopted after the resumption of peace in Europe in 1815.

This upsurge in activity locally is not surprising when viewed in the wider contexts of the accelerating growth rates which characterised the British economy during this period, and the development of manufacturing in many other parts of the North and Midlands. Nor, despite the popular association of the industrial revolution with urban growth, was industry's rural setting unusual. Even the textile heartland of south-east Lancashire was predominantly a landscape of factory villages, handloom weavers' settlements and mining colonies, 'presenting an appearance somewhat like a vast city scattered amongst meads and pastures, and belts of woodland'.[6] The scale of local enterprises and methods employed were also similar to those found elsewhere. Apart from the application of water power and mechanisation to the spinning of textiles, most manufacturing, like hatting, pottery, and basket-making, was carried out in workshops. It was labour-intensive and relied heavily on manual dexterity and primitive technology. Surface steam engines for pumping water were gradually installed at large underground coal mines after mid-century but most pits and quarries were operated by sub-contractors, who worked them in fits and starts rather than continuously.[7] Everywhere the laborious processes of excavating, extracting and transporting the country's mineral wealth relied on sweat and muscle.

There are specific reasons, however, why these particular industries became established in this green and pleasant valley during this period. All depended to some extent on exploiting natural resources either for raw materials or for power. All demonstrate the importance of local families, who provided either the initial capital investment or, like the Irelands of Arkholme (basket-making) or Batesons of Burton (pottery), were responsible for passing expertise down through the generations. However, rough distinctions can be drawn between extractive industries, small-scale workshops and textile manufacturing. The first two were primarily dependent on local resources and, less exclusively, on a regional market. The last looked overseas for raw materials and markets, and operated on a very different scale.

Mining and quarrying

The nature and extent of mineral deposits in the district were clearly important determinants of mining and quarrying. As Phil Hudson demonstrates, there were abundant supplies of stone in the area which had long been regularly exploited for a variety of purposes. The region's underlying geology also explains the intermittent, unstable and dispersed nature of coal mining. Until the very end of the nineteenth century when outside capital transformed the scale of operations around Ingleton and expanded brick making at Claughton, these extractive industries required little in the way of capital or specialist technical equipment. They relied essentially on picks and shovels, and on heavy manual labour. As in the rest of the country, local landowners were often important for providing the infrastructure at the larger pits, such as surface pumping engines and winding gear, but the extent of this initial investment locally was relatively limited and they often leased sites to others and played little role in marketing.

Until the late nineteenth century when rail opened up the market, particularly for limestone, extractive industries also relied primarily on local markets. Although high-quality building stone could be transported long distances, especially to London,[8] the market for Lune valley quarries did not stretch much beyond Lancaster. The poor quality of local coal, and the difficulties and cost of road transport, meant that this was also largely consumed locally, although Ingleton and Wray colliers sold as far afield as Kendal and Lancaster and expressed anxiety about the potential impact of the Preston to Kendal Canal on their trade.[9] In these early years, quarrying and mining were beneficiaries rather than engines of growth, supplying building materials, limestone for agricultural improvement, and fuel for domestic heating.

Workshop manufacturing

Small-scale manufacturing also re-lied to a considerable extent on local resources. The availability of shale and clay deposits largely explain the location of Burton in Lonsdale's pottery industry, although their rela-tively poor quality also limited its growth. Tile and, later, brickmaking at Claughton would not have been possible without the clay and shale deposits on Caton Moor. Hatting made use of local wool and rabbit fur, and basket- makers at Arkholme cultivated local osier beds. The small businesses engaged in these industries employed relatively un-sophisticated methods of production which required limited capital investment. Burton produced hand-thrown pottery which was being abandoned by the larger Staffordshire firms in favour of moulded ware during the late eighteenth century. Hat-making was a dirty, dangerous job which required little more than a kettle for heating the felt. As Emmeline Garnett's chapter vividly demonstrates, bas-ket-making required even less equipment, and depended almost entirely on repetitive manual labour. We know much less about nail making, other than that it was carried out in Wray, Masongill, Westhouse and Bentham. The trade at Wray was reported as being 'very brisk' employing a consider-able number of men, but here, as elsewhere, it was of 'small dimensions'

The Nailmaker: William Kenyon, and his wife Ann, photographed in their finery towards the end of their lives. William's father James is reputed to have been the first nailmaker in the village; William was the last. In 1861 he was living at 'Back of Beck', a terrace of cottages on the road to Roeburndale East. His workshop was a single storey building just to the west of these. (Courtesy of the Kenyon family, Wray)

The Joiner and Wheelwright: Mr Parker-Foxcroft, joiner and wheelwright, pictured in his workshop, adjacent to Ashley House, Main Street, Wray, sometime in the 1950s. At one time he employed several men and apprentices, some of whom continued, and continue, to work locally. (Courtesy of the Kenyon family, Wray)

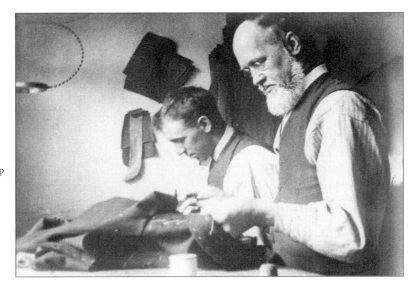

The Village Tailor: Richard Kenyon and his son Ronnie, working in basement of their premises, Roeburn House. Richard, a younger son of William, built these premises in the 1880s overlooking the river. They were later used as a grocer's shop but are now a private house. (Courtesy of the Kenyon family, Wray)

and carried out by petty tradesmen, none of them employing more than five to seven men.[10] This information fits what is known about it elsewhere in the country where it was a poor, relatively unskilled trade carried out in dispersed units of production.[11] Although individually these industries were not major players in the labour market or national economy, collectively they sustained the viability of small settlements such as Burton, Wray and Arkholme and their skills were frequently passed down through several generations of families who were often intermarried. In the case of hatting, as Christine Workman reveals, religious networks were also important for creating important business contacts which extended well beyond the region and which were very influential in determining the growth and subsequent demise of the industry.

The markets for these locally-produced goods were always more diverse than for minerals. Baskets and swills were widely used as household utensils but, since they were relatively easy to transport, they also enjoyed a market among fishermen around Morecambe Bay and farmers, particularly potato growers, at least as far south as the Fylde. Burton's slipware pottery was largely utilitarian in style and function and would initially appear to have been sold within a relatively limited area, but the development of railways later encouraged specialisation in stoneware for a much wider market. Hatters met local demands, but during their prosperous heyday they tapped into distant markets, exporting overseas and sending hat bases to London for finishing by high-class firms like Christy and Co.

Textiles and the maritime economy

The expansion of textile production in the late eighteenth century, particularly the expansion of water-powered mills described here by James Price, was heavily influenced by events outside the region. Entrepreneurs needed to possess detailed knowledge of potential sources of supplies since the raw materials for silk, cotton, linen and even worsted were not local, but distantly sourced. The scale of production employed was also substantially different from workshop industry. Both factory spinning and handloom weaving needed to attract, and retain, substantial labour forces. Fixed investment requirements were much higher: to acquire rights to extract water, erect or adapt premises, construct earthworks, and buy specialist machinery. Substantial working capital was needed to purchase raw materials, pay workers and provide extended credit to purchasers. Markets were national and international.

By the late eighteenth century textile production was rapidly beginning to dominate the West Riding and south-east Lancashire, but local firms did not begin life as outliers of these regional centres. Rather they were part of an integrated maritime economy which stretched from Liverpool, the commercial capital of the North West, up to southern Scotland, incorporating Lancaster, Whitehaven and a host of smaller ports.[12] The sea, not the turnpike roads and canals which feature so prominently in most textbooks, was the commercial artery through which trade was pumped around the region. Beyond this it provided access to London and, even more importantly, the world, including North America and Africa. Particularly important in this context were the region's close connections with colonies in the West Indies, whose islands dominated the importation of cotton wool into Britain until the early 1800s and accounted for as much as 30% of cotton exports and 80% of linen exports in the late eighteenth century, and with Baltic ports which supplied much of the flax and hemp for linen and rope production.[13] For much of the eighteenth century textile manufacturers also benefited from government policies which deliberately sought to promote overseas trade by limiting foreign competition in colonial and domestic markets through import duties and export bounties, with the linen industry further benefiting from the stipulation that English shipping had to carry sailcloth which had been woven exclusively in England.

Although there were examples of small-scale partnerships at Catshaw and Ingleton, here, as elsewhere in the North West, the expansion of textiles 'did not provide unprecedented opportunities for the small man'.[14] Rather, expansion into cotton, silk and worsted was spearheaded by a relatively small number of substantial merchant-manufacturers, usually sons of local yeomen or farming families, most of whom had already made their money from overseas trade.[15] Their influence stretched as far north as Sedbergh where Robert Foster, the son of the prominent West Indian merchant Dodshon Foster, founded a woollen mill around 1790 and east to Bentham and Ingleton.[16] Prominent linen merchants and manufacturers also expanded into the valley, initially to recruit handloom weavers, especially around Bentham and Burton, to supplement their existing workforces, but then to establish mills. Henry Smithies of Bela Mill, Milnthorpe, 'flax and tow spinners, rope twine, bed tick, wrappers and sacking manufacturers', for example, owned the mill at Burton in Lonsdale until the early 1840s.[17] James Coates, a linen manufacturer of Kirkby Lonsdale, operated the spinning mill at Ingleton from 1813.[18]

Furthermore, the activities of such men clearly demonstrate 'the basis of eighteenth-century networking founded on family and religious ties' through which additional credit, knowledge and trustworthy business partners could be obtained.[19] Within the region's small, close-knit business community, inter-marriage and shared belief further bolstered the confidence to invest, provided the means to succeed and frequently determined how businesses changed hands. These family connections are potentially bewildering in their complexity and their full extent and potential significance are still being uncovered by painstaking research by local historians. It is only possible here to illustrate some of the links in the chain which held this business community together.

Thomas and John Hodgson, who established the first cotton mills in Caton, were younger sons of a local yeoman who made their fortunes by speculating in trade, including West African slavery, operating initially from Lancaster but subsequently from Liverpool. When the family eventually disposed of Low Mill, they did so to Thomas's brother-in-law, Samuel Greg, a cotton magnate from Quarry Bank Mill, Styal, who also had extensive investments in, and connections with, West Indian plantations.[20] James Noble, who built Rumble Mill, Caton about 1788 on land initially leased

Escowbeck Hall, Caton: Not a country landowner's residence, but the new mansion built by *c.* 1842 by John Greg, who owned mills in Caton and on Moor Lane, Lancaster. He sold them to Storeys in the 1860s. The sender of this particular postcard commented, 'There is a lake at the foot of the card where we feed the ducks and skate in winter. Is this not pretty?' (*Lancaster City Museums*)

from the Hodgsons, was a silk merchant in Lancaster, as were his partners at Galgate silk mill, John Armstrong and William Thompson.[21]

Another successful local family, the Hindes took over Dolphinholme mill in the mid-1790s. Thomas Hinde's father, also Thomas, had traded through Lancaster and Liverpool and amassed a fortune from the African and West Indian trade.[22] His son, another Thomas, and his daughter Jane, married offspring of Thomas Mason, a West Indian merchant and shipowner who, in partnership with Thomas Burrow, had financed the first cotton mill in Lancaster in 1802. Thomas Mason junior, usually described as a solicitor, was jointly responsible for building Ridge Lane silk mill in 1837 which was then let to a Walter Hinde, who also later ran the mill at Wray.[23] Meanwhile Thomas Burrow's son George had teamed up with his brother-in-law Thomas Higgin, son of the castle governor, to build a mill on Moor Lane. The Burrow name also appears in Baines' trade directory of 1825 in partnership with Robinson at Halton mill.[24] John Swainson, who took this over in 1834, was descended through his mother's line from the Inman family, yet another important family involved in trade and shipowning, one of whom had married George Burrow's sister. Yet another Burrow, also George, had erected a cotton mill in the family's home village of Westhouse, briefly owned the mill at Ingleton and had interests in a weaving shed at Austwick.[25]

Investment in the linen industry was dominated by a small coterie of inter-linked family dynasties. The Hornbys' empire originated from Kirkham on the Fylde and was initially built on sailcloth. They operated in Low Bentham from around 1785, and at High Bentham from c. 1803 to 1850. At High Mill they were initially in partnership with Charles Parker who had been responsible for starting the mill there in the 1790s.[26] Parker, was a Quaker. He had married into the wealthy Quaker Waithman family of Yealand, flax merchants who, with Parker, had established the mill at Holme near Milnthorpe. John Kendrew, whose family originally hailed from Wyresdale and who was responsible for patenting the first flax spinning machine at Darlington in 1787, was Parker's brother-in-law, also by marriage into the Waithmans. In 1851 the Hornbys sold both mills in Bentham to the Waithmans who continued to operate them until their financial difficulties in 1866 let to their takeover by a new company, Bentham Mills Ltd, whose shareholders included leading Quakers such as Joseph Rowntree of York. The Quakers' personal connections with Bentham continued into the twentieth century, when Benson Ford took over Low Mill in 1877 for silk spinning. Although he was born and educated outside the district, members of the Ford family were also neighbours of the Waithmans in Yealand.[27]

Although these wealthy families' names featured prominently in the titles of firms from the outset, they differed from small workshop businesses in that in many cases they delegated the responsibility for the daily management of factories to others. Several of these became successful men in their own right. The Hodgsons had a partner at Low Mill, Isaac Capstick, who described himself as a cotton spinner and later teamed up at Forge Mill with James Bradshaw, another Lancaster merchant. At Willow Mill the Hodgsons were partnered by Robert Hadwen, flax spinner and sailcloth manufacturer of Lancaster. At Dolphinholme Thomas Derham, the son of a Lancaster warehouseman who was involved in the putting out domestic system, was hired as manager. His son James was subsequently taken into the firm as a partner, operating as Hinde and Derham. Robert Foster in Sedbergh brought in Joseph Dover, a hosier from Keswick, who later operated mills under his own name. In the 1840s John Greg & Co's mills on Moor Lane were supervised by a 'managing partner', Robert Bickerdike, and Caton Low Mill was run Henry Baker. In the same period William Stubbs and William Watson managed Thompson's silk mills at Caton and Galgate respectively.

Stagnation and decline

By middle of the nineteenth century, however, the conditions which had spawned the expansion of the rural industry in the valley had largely disappeared and with them the rationale for the initial location of many of its enterprises disappeared. Those which survived increasingly did so as part of industries whose centres of gravity lay elsewhere, particularly in Yorkshire. The men who took over the reins of industry from the merchant families and Quaker dynasties also increasingly came from industrial backgrounds and relied on other, less personal sources of capital.

Reasons for the failure of the area to maintain its earlier momentum in textiles are complex and, as yet, little explored or understood.[28] Changing patterns of international and domestic trade, in particular the eclipse of the West Indies as a major supplier of cotton and purchaser of manufactured goods, were clearly important, as were Liverpool's growing connections with more developed centres of industry elsewhere in the North and Midlands. Flax spinning contracted rapidly once the original favourable conditions which had led to the expansion of overseas trade had disappeared after the Napoleonic Wars. Ingleton flax mill was converted to cotton by the late 1830s and the Hornbys transferred their investments to cotton further south in the county from the 1850s. Factories in Burton in Lonsdale and Ingleton were converted from flax spinning to cotton and limped along on until the closing decades of the century. Local cotton manufacturers, however, suffered from their inability to benefit from the external economies of scale which firms in south-east Lancashire enjoyed and from their distance from Manchester which had consolidated its commercial stranglehold over distribution. Cotton ceased to be spun in the smaller mills such as Catshaw and Westhouse around the middle of the century. Calder Vale survived under its original owners until the 1880s, and exceptionally continues to weave cloth today.[29] Worsted production at Dolpinholme never recovered from the collapse of Hinde and Derham in the depression of 1839 when their firm crashed with debts of £250,000, although by then the mill was but a small part of their business empire which was largely centred in and around Leeds.[30]

Mills which survived beyond mid-century did so by attracting a different breed of entrepreneurs, often from outside the immediate district. Dolphinholme mill was converted to cotton in the 1840s and run by Preston firms until closure in 1869. John Greg, whose family who had extensive cotton enterprises elsewhere in the North West,[31] was responsible for rebuilding Low Mill in Caton, but other mills in the village which did not attract outside capital were turned over to less labour-intensive bobbin production by the 1860s. From the 1860s both Low Mill, Caton and the mills at Halton, were incorporated into Lancaster's expanding oilcloth industry.

Silk spinners were adversely affected by the opening up of the British market to French imports after 1860 and local mills only survived by cementing connections with the major centre of waste silk spinning in the West Riding. Galgate mill was rescued after 1869 by the injection of Yorkshire capital and skilled labour. After the First World War it was taken over by a group of West Riding businessmen. Wray mill was operated until 1869 by the Hindes, but on their demise it was purchased by a Yorkshire firm, Davies & Co., who specialised in the production of dressed silk for spinning elsewhere.[32] By the 1890s, however, the mill had ceased production. The chief beneficiary of its demise, and a possible cause of it, was Benson Ford's, later Ford Ayrton's, silk spinning business at Low Bentham which had transferred production there from west Yorkshire in 1877.[33]

The smaller local industries enjoyed mixed fortunes. Hatting's precipitous decline was bound up with the collapsing market for felt hats from the 1830s, but its fate had already been largely determined by Christy's decision to concentrate its northern production around Stockport and to withdraw from Wray in 1822. The establishment of a rail network in the region from the 1840s did not necessarily enhance business prospects. The chief beneficiaries of cheap rail transport were bulk producers, especially the large-scale quarrying and mining concerns around Ingleton, the iron works at Carnforth, and brick and tile making at Claughton. Many smaller local quarries, however, suffered. Demand for Backsbottom's stone roofing slates, for example, declined in the face of imports of lighter slate from the Lake District and North Wales. Mining of the 'Lonsdale coals' at Tatham, Farleton, Caton and Roeburndale did not survive much beyond the 1840s, although the larger Smear Hall colliery only closed in the 1880s. Further north, the opening of the Settle to Carlisle railway inflicted a similar blow to mining in Dentdale. Arkholme's basket-makers were better able to market their products beyond the immediate vicinity, but Burton's earthenwares faced fiercer competition in their traditional markets from superior goods brought in from the Staffordshire Potteries. The local firms responded, however, by developing new markets further afield for new stoneware products, particularly spirits jars and jampots.

Improved rail communication further served to undermine the importance of the maritime economy and rural industry's dependence on Lancaster and the coast by opening up connections with other parts of the country. This was particularly evident in the upper Lune Valley, especially around Bentham and Ingleton. The mining and quarrying industries there increasingly attracted Yorkshire finance and found their markets to the east. Textile producers, too, increasingly looked away from the coast. Prior to the 1840s both the Hornbys and the Waithmans had been committed to the maritime economy. Both families were shareholders in the Lancaster Steam Navigation Company which built the steam packet for the Liverpool service in 1824.[34] They stored imported flax on St George's Quay in Lancaster and transported it by road or canal to their mills. After 1846, however, the Waithmans could bypass Lancaster and bring flax directly from Liverpool by rail to their mills at Holme. After 1850 their Bentham mills could also obtain flax directly from east coast ports.[35] The Lancaster to Leeds railway also cemented links between silk spinners at Galgate and Bentham with the centre of the industry around Leeds and Halifax. By the end of the century, therefore, with the notable exceptions of Halton and Caton, the valley's textile industry had few connections with Lancaster and the coast.

Old Quarry, Moorside, Caton: This wooded valley remains little changed today but, as the postcard's caption makes clear, the site was once very different. Traces of its earlier purposes can still be discerned in the valley floor. (*Lancaster City Museums*)

The people of Lunesdale

The consequences of this industrial growth and subsequent contraction for the inhabitants of the valley were profound. In common with many other parts of the country, the area witnessed a population explosion in the closing decades of the eighteenth century. Although some of this can be attributed to increasing demand for labour created by the shift from pastoral to arable farming in the late eighteenth century, and by related investment in agricultural improvement by landowners, industrial expansion was clearly also important, especially in the more substantial settlements such as Bentham, Wray, Burton, Caton and Halton. The employment opportunities for young people in textiles and extractive industries removed the barriers to marriage which dependence on the land had imposed and helped to curtail the exodus of family members who had previously been surplus to requirements. Precise figures are unavailable before the first decennial census in 1801, but parish registers which have survived for certain townships clearly show a marked increase in the excess of births over deaths from the 1750s which widened still further after the 1770s suggesting that some of the population increase was caused by a trend towards earlier marriage and larger families.[36] However, people were also undoubtedly attracted into the area by the prospect of well-paid family employment. Joseph Shaw, whose son Benjamin has left us a remarkable written record of the family's activities, was one such person who was persuaded to uproot his family from Dentdale to the new mill at Dolphinholme in 1791, along with many others, on hearing 'a fine tale what good wages we could get'.[37] Between 1801 and 1821 the rapid expansion of rural industry meant that virtually every rural township recorded rates of population increase well in excess of nearby Lancaster.

TABLE 1.1 Population change in the Lune Valley, 1801–1891

	Percentage Decennial Change		
	Lancaster District	Lower Lune (above Lancaster)	Kirkby Lonsdale
1801–11	1.09	6.74	6.63
1811–21	9.36	19.69	20.10
1821–31	20.68	−5.99	2.62
1831–41	12.90	−5.67	−3.38
1841–51	3.01	4.68	2.82
1851–61	0.59	−7.67	3.10
1861–71	18.76	−6.46	2.26
1871–81	27.39	−4.20	−1.87
1881–91	29.89	−5.52	3.98

Calculated from published decennial Census Tables.

But the population boom was shortlived. After the 1820s as the fortunes of these industries either fluctuated or declined dramatically, the local labour market deteriorated. The most dramatic collapse in numbers occurred in troubled Hornby township (including Farleton), where the population plummeted from 568 to 380 in just twenty years. The historian Edwin Butterworth, visiting the township in 1836 as Edward Baines's research assistant, found it 'a declining and desolate town, neglected by its Lords, possessing no trade and scarce any passing traffic – there are no motives or means for improvement'.[38] But declining numbers were evident elsewhere in the valley, and throughout rural Britain by this time, as industrialisation became increasingly synonymous with urbanisation. The populations of Gressingham, Melling, Hornby, Roeburndale, Tatham, Halton, Tunstall, Over Kellet, Nether Kellet, Thornton in Lonsdale, Burton in Lonsdale and Clapham all achieved nineteenth-century peaks in 1821. Numbers also fell dramatically from the 1830s in settlements on the upper reaches of the Lune such as Barbon, Middleton and Firbank, the slide relieved only by temporary influxes of railway navvies in 1861 and 1871. The market towns of Sedbergh and Kirkby Lonsdale were boosted somewhat by the presence of local boarding schools and the custom of local gentry, but they, too, witnessed steady declines in the number of permanent inhabitants in the late nineteenth century.

With the exception of Bentham, where the population has remained remarkably stable over 150 years, the valley's main industrial settlements experienced violent fluctuations in numbers throughout the nineteenth century. Halton's population rose from 776 in 1811 to 1027 in 1821 before collapsing dramatically to 834 only ten years later. Numbers in Wray oscillated from just 586 in 1831 to 833 twenty years later, before falling erratically to fewer than 500 by the end of the century. A contemporary account of 1890 vividly conjured up the transformation in the village's fortunes.

> The appearances in the street are greatly changed. The moving about of the workmen and the noise and din of a busy multitude have passed like that of an exhausted storm. The merry song and laughter of the hatters, and the almost incessant singular noise from the preparing of material for hat manufacture, are no longer heard in the street. The colliers going to work at early morn sucking their Indian weed from short black pipes, carrying their newly sharpened picks, their food and their bottles of cold tea, and arrayed in tattered garments suitable for coal mining – all this is a picture of the past. The clatter of nailmakers' hammers, and the 'puff-puff' of grimy bellows, are no longer heard in the streets. The packing of hats, nails, and other manufactured materials, the loading of carts and other vehicles to carry away the produce of the village industries are all gone. All the noise and push of extinct industries have subsided into a stillness almost like desolation. Now at times one might stand at the Cross and look down the street west and east and not see a living being of man, woman, child, cat or dog.[39]

Notes in the published census tables occasionally provided explanations for exceptional falls in population elsewhere. In 1831 the decrease in Thornton in Lonsdale was attributed to 'families migrating in search of work'; in Hornby 'to families having left for the manufacturing districts'; in Roeburndale to 'the failure of a colliery'; and in Wray to 'declining state of trade'. Further declines in populations in 1851 were also attributed to the failure of industry. In Bentham it was 'the cessation of work at a linen factory'. In Ellel the large number of empty houses was 'in consequence of a woollen factory being unoccupied', while in Sedbergh 'emigration and the stoppage of a cotton mill' were blamed. Twenty years later the 'depression in the silk trade' and the closing of a silk mill' were given as the causes of the decreases in Ellel and Wray.

These, then, were not stable industrial communities. Although there are still people in the area who can trace their families back to the eighteenth century or beyond, the fact that the number of births in the area has exceeded deaths for most of the nineteenth and twentieth centuries while population has stagnated or declined is indicative of a significant rural exodus. Entire families could disappear between censuses, even during periods of apparent prosperity and growth. Around half of those present in Caton in 1841 were not there ten years later; and half of the families present in 1851 had also gone by 1861. The young were particularly prone to leave. Where they went remains unclear. Gooderson identified a considerable number of Caton-born living in Lancaster in 1851 and 1861, with a preponderance of women, many of them married to Lancaster men. He surmised that men went further afield, but we do not know for sure. Over the course of the century, therefore, the valley exported not just cotton,

W. Thompson & Co, Galgate Mill, c. 1905: Silk doublers and winders. Although the skilled silk dressers were adult males, a significant number coming from Yorkshire during the 1870s, most of the mill workers were young females. These generally gave up work when they got married and often left the village. (*Lancaster City Museums*)

Ford Ayrton's works' outing: As this smiling group of employees implies, Ford Ayrton adopted a paternalistic attitude towards its workers throughout its history. (*Lancaster City Museums*)

silk, coal, pots, baskets and hats, it exported people. For many children and adolescents, growing up in the Lune Valley involved preparing themselves, mentally and emotionally, to leave it.[40]

The tendency for people to migrate in search of work when trade was depressed must have added to the problems which local businesses faced from the late nineteenth century, particularly when they attempted to expand or to revive their operations after a period of depression. The uncertain nature of the employment and the limited prospects for promotion which were natural corollaries of small-scale industrial enterprises meant that employers found it increasingly difficult to recruit and retain skilled labour. The injection of Yorkshire capital attracted significant numbers of silk dressers to Galgate in the 1870s but in most cases when workers came any distance they did so under the aegis of employers' initiatives. This was particularly evident in Bentham. The Hornbys are known to have brought workers with them from Kirkham in the late eighteenth and early nineteenth centuries. The Waithmans attracted families from south Westmorland in the 1850s, including several of Irish descent. Ford Ayrton's arrival in Low Bentham drew in workers from the smaller, struggling mill in neighbouring Wray but the firm relied on skilled workers and managers who migrated with the firm from Leeds.

It was not just skilled workers who could be in short supply. Many of the juveniles and young adults initially employed in textiles were members of households whose heads depended on coalmining, hatting, nailmaking or agricultural labour. Declining opportunities for adult males in these sectors of the local economy later in the nineteenth century, therefore, further tended to deplete the supply of younger workers. In extreme cases pauper orphans were employed. The Hodgsons at Caton recruited them from workhouses in Lancaster, London and Liverpool as early as the 1780s. Ford Ayrton's adopted a virtually identical tactic over a century later, bringing in young, female orphans from Liverpool although, interestingly, in stark contrast to historians' general condemnation of earlier child labour, this practice has generally been praised as being philanthropic.[41]

Such influxes, however, were exceptional and their effects short-lived. In most of the townships of the Lune Valley, from Ravenstonedale right down to Claughton and up along the tributaries of the Wenning, Hindburn, Greta and Roeburn, there were fewer residents in late twentieth century than there were in the early nineteenth. In many cases the collapse in numbers has been simply stunning. Roeburndale could muster just 67 people in 1971 compared to 237 at its peak 150 years earlier; Tatham had 337 as opposed to 765 in 1821; Wray 401 as opposed to 833 in 1851. It would be wrong to attribute all of this collapse to the retreat of industry; smaller families and the shedding of agricultural labour have been equally, if not more important from the late nineteenth century, but the lack of industrial employment has certainly been a major contributory factor.

The valley today

Although a number of rural businesses survived well into the twentieth century, in some cases only closing in the 1960s and 1970s, the heady days of expansion were then but a distant memory. Today little remains in the way of significant industry in the district and what there is is mainly controlled by large international companies. High Bentham is the only settlement offering significant employment in manufacturing, although numbers have fallen substantially in recent years. Brick making in Claughton is also a remarkable survival which, despite its prestigious owners and high-quality product, still relies on an overhead pulley system which is nearly a century old to bring its raw materials down from Caton Moor. Large-scale quarrying by multinational conglomerates is all too evident around Ingleton and south of Carnforth. Elsewhere there are a few light industrial estates. There are also some local crafts, although nowhere near to the same extent as in Cumbria or the Yorkshire Dales. Tourism is now the major 'industry', but the craft shops in centres such as Kirkby Lonsdale increasingly sell products sourced elsewhere, in many cases outside the country.

Despite the lack of local employment, however, population levels in some parts of the valley have soared since the 1950s as the spread of car ownership has enabled incomers to combine country living with urban employment, or encouraged others to retire to the area. Between 1951 and 1971 Halton's population rose by nearly 150%, Caton's doubled, and Hornby's shot up by 50% as new housing developments transformed their appearance and function. Wray village street is again busy with traffic. The appeal of the area, however, is now very different than it was a century and a half ago. Then, residents' survival was dependent on the prospect of local employment in agriculture, quarrying, hatting, mining, or mill work. Now, only a small minority find work in farming, and it is the very absence of the other industries which attracts residential incomers. Attempts to revive lost industries, or to introduce their modern equivalents, to provide significant local employment could well provoke significant opposition from environmental and residential lobbies. For permanent residents and passing visitors alike, far more so than it ever was in Turner's day, it is the 'perfect landscape of the extensive sort' which is the area's major asset, but, as the following chapters demonstrate, it is a landscape which still bears the marks of its industrial past.

Notes

I am grateful to members of Wray Local History Study Group for comments on an earlier draft of this introduction.

1. The focus throughout the book is on the Lune and its tributaries above Lancaster, with some information drawn from neighbouring Wyresdale. The development of industry in Lancaster itself and along the coast, although influenced by some of the factors discussed here, followed a rather different trajectory.
2. M. Humphries, 'The Development and Decline of Industry in the Ancient Parishes of Bentham and Thornton in Lonsdale in the Nineteenth Century', Unpublished Local History Diploma Dissertation, Liverpool University (in Lancaster Univ. Library), 1984, p. 4 quoting the unpublished work of John Bentley on Elizabethan Ingleton.
3. M. Robinson, 'The Linen Industry of North-West England, 1660–1830', Unpublished PhD Thesis, Lancaster University, 1997, chapter 8. See also her chapter, 'The Linen Industry in North Lancashire and Cumbria, 1660–1830', in E. Roberts, *A History of Linen in the North West* (CNWRS, 1998), pp. 44–65.
4. Hornby Castle Sederunt, 31 August, 1751, Lancaster Reference Library, MS 1533, pp. 21–23. I am grateful to Jennifer Holt and Emmeline Garnett for this reference.
5. For further information on the history of Burton potteries see H. Bateson, 'The Potteries of Burton-in-Lonsdale (or Black Burton), *Yorkshire History Quarterly*, vol. 5, no. 2, October 1999, pp. 60–5; Humphries, 'Industry in Lonsdale', p. 25; A. White, *Country Pottery from Burton in Lonsdale* (Lancaster City Museums, Local Studies, 1989). A detailed study of the potteries is currently being prepared by Phil Hudson and Henry Bateson.
6. S. Bamford, *Walks in South Lancashire and on its Borders* (1844, reprinted Harvester Press, Brighton, 1972), p. 10.
7. R. Samuel, 'Mineral Workers', in R. Samuel (ed.), *Miners, Quarrymen and Saltworkers* (Routledge & Kegan Paul, 1977), p. 32.
8. Samuel, 'Mineral Workers', p. 14.
9. Humphries, 'Industry in Lonsdale', pp. 18–9.
10. *Lancaster Guardian*, 16 March 1890 (Decayed Industries of Wray); Joseph Carr, *Bygone Bentham* (Landy Publishing, Blackpool, 1997), p. 59 (7 December 1893).
11. M. Berg, *The Age of Manufactures, 1700–1870* (Routledge, London, 1994), p. 268.

12. See, for example, R. K. Bingham, *The Chronicles of Milnthorpe* (Cicerone Press, Milnthorpe, 1987), p. 163. The region's close connections with Liverpool, London and Ireland are in need of further investigation and may well transform our understanding of regional development during the period. For some ideas on the significance of this see M. Robinson, '"An Intercourse of Trade": Coastal Shipping in the North West', *CNWRS Bulletin*, new series, 13, 1999, pp. 30–7; V. Burton, 'Liverpool's Mid-Nineteenth Century Coastal Trade', in V. Burton (ed.), *Liverpool Shipping, Trade and Industry* (Merseyside Museums and Galleries, 1989), pp. 26–67. There is also much scattered evidence associated with cotton, hatting, furniture, agricultural produce and banking which suggests strong London links.

13. M. M. Edwards, *The Growth of the British Cotton Trade, 1780–1815* (Manchester University Press, 1967), pp. 250–1; Robinson, 'Linen Industry', pp. 279–90.

14. K. Honeyman, *Origins of Enterprise: Business Leadership in the Industrial Revolution* (Manchester University Press, 1982), p. 69.

15. S. Chapman, 'The Commercial Sector', in M. B. Rose (ed.), *The Lancashire Cotton Industry: A History since 1700* (Lancashire County Books, 1996), pp. 63–72.

16. W. Thompson, *Sedbergh, Garsdale and Dent* (Richard Jackson, Leeds, 1892), p. 180; *Sedbergh and District History Society Newsletter*, February 1983, p. 6. I am grateful to Joyce Scobie of Sedbergh for this information. On the Fosters see M. Elder, 'Dodshon Foster of Lancaster', *Lancaster Maritime Journal*, 1, 1997, pp. 14–9 and *The Slave Trade and the Economic Development of Eighteenth-Century Lancaster* (Halifax: Ryburn, 1992), pp. 127–8.

17. Bingham, *Milnthorpe*, pp. 164–5; Humphries, 'Industry in Lonsdale', p. 38.

18. Humphries, 'Industry in Lonsdale', pp. 41–2.

19. Robinson, 'Linen Industry' , p. 356.

20. M. B. Rose, *The Gregs of Quarry Bank Mill* (Manchester University Press, 1986), pp. 25, 38–9.

21. P. J. Gooderson, 'The Social and Economic History of Caton, 1750–1914', Unpublished MA Dissertation, Lancaster University, 1969, p. 29; Elder, *Slave Trade*, p. 188.

22. P. P. Hall, *Dolphinholme: a History of Dolphinholme Worsted Mill, 1784–1867* reprinted from *Transactions of the Fylde Historical Society*, 3, 1969, pp. 6–7; Elder, *Slave Trade*, pp. 141–2, 188.

23. P. H. S. McCann, 'A Comparative Study of Halton and Wray, Two Water-Powered Industrial Communities in the Lune Valley, c. 1700 to 1900', Unpublished MA Dissertation, Lancaster University, 1969, pp. 15–6.

24. M. M. Schofield, *Outlines of an Economic History of Lancaster from 1680 to 1860; Part II, 1800–1860* (Lancaster Branch of the Historical Association, 1951), p. 112; Humphries, 'Industry in Lonsdale', pp. 35–6.

25. I am grateful to Geoff Brown of Westhouse for information on the Burrow family, and to Margaret Bainbridge of Lancaster for details on the Burrows, Hindes and Masons. Michael Wright, 'The Inman Family of Lancaster and Hill House, Silverdale', *The Mourholme Magazine of Local History*, 1999–2000, 2, pp. 6–16.

26. The Hornbys were also in partnership with other families and had establishments in Cumbria. For further details, see Robinson, *passim*, and J. Wilkinson, 'The Linen Merchant-Manufacturers of Kirkham in the Eighteenth and Nineteenth Centuries', in Roberts, *Linen in the North West*, pp. 66–92.

27. Carr, *Bygone Bentham*, p. 129.
28. The best survey of this period is D. M. Clark, 'The Economic and Social Geography of Rural Lonsdale, 1801–1861', Unpublished MA Thesis, University of Liverpool, 1968.
29. Humphries, 'Industry in Lonsdale', pp. 38–42; J. Wilcock, *A Lancashire Industrial Village Survives: The Story of Calder Vale and Oakenclough* (the author, printed by Colin Cross, Garstang, 1997).
30. D. T. Jenkins & K. G. Ponting, *The British Wool Textile Industry, 1770–1914* (Scolar Press/Pasold Trust, 1982), p. 127.
31. Rose, *Gregs*, passim.
32. Henry Davies, silk manufacturer employing 65 workers was resident at Roeburn House in Wray in 1881.
33. E. R. & J. P. Pafford, *Employer and Employed: Ford Ayrton & Co. Ltd 1870–1970* (Pasold Research Fund, 1974).
34. Schofield, *Economic History, Part II*, p. 24; Robinson 'Linen Industry', pp. 354–63; Humphries, 'Industry in Lonsdale', pp. 48–52.
35. Schofield, *Economic History*, Part II, p. 24.
36. Clark, 'Rural Lonsdale'; Humphries, 'Industry in Lonsdale', p. 36; McCann, 'Wray and Halton', pp. 20–3; Gooderson, 'Caton', pp. 5–8.
37. A. Crosby (ed.), *The Family Records of Benjamin Shaw, Mechanic of Dent, Dolphinholme and Preston, 1772–1841* (Record Society of Lancashire and Cheshire, vol. CXXX, 1991), pp. 6–7.
38. Edwin Butterworth MSS, Oldham Local Studies Library, D-BUT/A/1/35/2, Notes on Melling Parish. Edward Baines published a two volume history of Lancashire in 1836. For Hornby's troubles during this period see E. Garnett, *John Marsden's Will: the Hornby Castle Dispute, 1780–1840* (Hambledon Press, London, 1998).
39. *Lancaster Guardian*, 16 March 1890.
40. Gooderson, 'Caton', pp. 6–9.
41. M. B. Rose, 'Social Policy and Business: Parish Apprenticeship and the Early Factory System', *Business History*, 31, 1990, pp. 5–32; Paffords, *Employer and Employed*, pp. 22–3.

CHAPTER TWO

Domestic Textile Production in the Sixteenth and Seventeenth Centuries

Barbara Pidcock

From the late sixteenth century, significant parts of the North West were already becoming involved in intensive textile production.[1] Kendal was developing its serges and bays, east Lancashire its kerseys and south Lancashire its linens and, later, fustians. The intention of this chapter was to investigate the extent of activity in the Lune Valley through an analysis of probate inventories and wills for parishes shown on the map below. At first sight the area seemed promising. There was ready access to fleece, linen and hemp, abundant water power, and a market and port in nearby Lancaster which was itself engaged in linen and canvas sail-cloth manufacture. Early Hornby Castle Estate accounts show evidence of fulling mills. A survey of 1582 records the sale of combed wool, and payments made for having 54 yards of harden woven up to make privy jackets.[2]

Yet, despite this, a sweep through 628 probate inventories yielded very meagre pickings. We shall look at the details of this search in later sections but, for the moment, suffice it to say that it would appear difficult from these results to show any significant kind of textile activity compared with the Colne Chapelry, the Pendle Forest and Kendal, three well-known textile producing areas during the period. The Lune Valley records showed very little in the way of textile equipment, stocks of wool, yarns or cloth, no obvious congregation of weavers in any one area and, apart from one instance, no sign of the activity of chapmen or middlemen. Only 2% of the sample had looms compared to 44% in Colne and 37% in Pendle, while 13% had spinning wheels, compared to 54% in Colne and 76% in Pendle. (This latter figure also included references to cards and combs.) It came nowhere near Kendal which had 133 of the principal 257 householders (52%) involved in textile-related occupations in 1695.[3] The Lune Valley seemed to have much more in common with the Ribble Valley and Furness Peninsula, similarly placed agricultural areas with no discernible industrial textile history until the mid-eighteenth century when, for example, linen and cotton spinning emerged in Ulverston and up the Crake Valley. Swain found just 23% of households with spinning wheels and 7% with looms in the Ribble Valley. A survey of similar records for Furness as late as the 1670s showed just 3% of households with looms and 25% with spinning wheels.[4]

This lack of evidence of substantial textile production for the market, however, is perhaps not surprising. Unlike the east Lancashire uplands, where a secondary occupation, such as textile production, was necessary for survival, the main reaches of Lune Valley were fertile, with abundant pasture, arable and woodland. Yet to find so little sign of even a local *domestic* industry, does not make a great deal of sense. After food and shelter, textiles were central in the life of all people, and rural people particularly had the means at hand to provide for their basic needs. They had sheep, hemp and flax and the skills needed to deal with these raw materials. In these circumstances, the well-known opening to Jane Austen's novel, *Pride and Prejudice*, that 'It is a truth universally acknowledged, that a single man in possession of a good fortune, must be in want of a wife', needs but little adaptation to appreciate the underlying drift of this argument. A man whatever his fortune needed a woman who could spin.

In an age when every thread of the cloth needed to clothe and furnish the nation had to be spun, woven or knitted by hand, would it not be reasonable to assume that a woman with access to fleece or fibres would be able to spin? – and a country woman would almost certainly have that access. Even if she had no sheep, or fibre crop herself, she could barter or

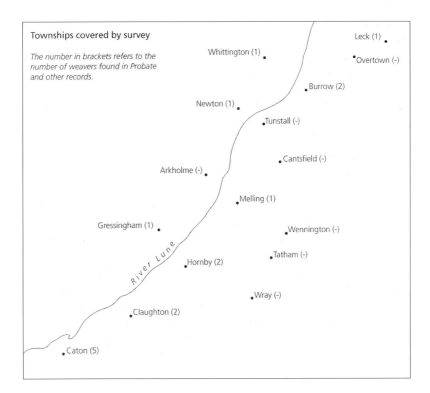

Townships covered by survey

The number in brackets refers to the number of weavers found in Probate and other records.

Leck (1)

Whittington (1)

Overtown (-)

Burrow (2)

Newton (1)

Tunstall (-)

Cantsfield (-)

Arkholme (-)

Melling (1)

Gressingham (1)

Wennington (-)

River Lune

Tatham (-)

Hornby (2)

Wray (-)

Claughton (2)

Caton (5)

sell her spinning skill to obtain the wool or hemp she needed for her own use. Weaving, too, being a primitive craft, is likely to have been carried out in a few cottages in the community, even if only at a very basic level. A woman who could spin her own yarn, and have it woven up locally for a few pence, is unlikely to take the trouble of walking to her nearest market, maybe half a day away, to spend good money on a length of cloth, which might be of no better quality than she could have provided for herself on her own doorstep.

Even better-off yeomen's and skilled craftsmen's families, who could have afforded higher quality 'Scotch' and 'Yorkshire' cloths available at the market, would probably have engaged in some production. Research on Furness has shown that the minor gentry, too, produced their own yarn, and had it woven up locally to supply clothes for farm and household servants, as well as sacking and other common domestic cloths. Nicolson and Burn, writing in 1777, considered that Westmorland people 'had departed of late years from their ancient simplicity. Their forefathers were wont to cloath themselves with their own wool manufactured at home.'[5] But, even in the late eighteenth century, other observers commented on the ubiquity of domestic cloth production. Sir Frederic Eden, for example, writing in 1797, considered that almost every article of dress, except shoes and hats, were made at home.[6] The unpublished reminiscences of Miss Isabella Greenbank Dobson of Caton, written from 1863, remembered in her youth 'four Miss Turners ... They had a room fitted up at the top of the house, where they used to spin for hire as all the yeoman's daughters at that time did.'[7]

The purpose of the chapter, therefore, is to consider whether in a rural area such as the Lune Valley, with access to wool and/or fibre crops, spinning and weaving of a basic nature took place, making the local people self-sufficient in basic essentials at least, with surplus raw materials possibly sent to market to sell to the specialist producers in the town, who used their skills and time in a different way. To do this, we have to look at what little evidence we have more rigorously, looking deeper under the surface and recognising, too, that the absence of mention of equipment does not prove there was no activity.

Altogether, 332 of the inventories (53% of the sample) contained references which could be interpreted as evidence of *possible* textile production, that is, listings of yarn, fibre, crops of linen and hemp and sheep as well as equipment such as looms, spinning wheels, cards and shears. (Table 2.1) Those showing only cloth holdings are also listed as an indication of how much cloth was held by local households. Table 2.2 looks more closely at the 158 inventories (25% of the sample) which listed textile equipment, and breaks them down into further categories. We shall now look at these in greater detail, going through the textile producing processes in order.

TABLE 2.1 Number of inventories showing any textile references
as defined above = 332 (53%)

	Category	No of references
a	Textile Equipment	158
b	Sheep	228
c	Fibres as crop or unspun	213
d	Spun yarn (wool/hemp/flax)	60
e	Fibres and yarn spun together	85
f	Cloth	76

TABLE 2.2 Number of inventories showing textile equipment

Item	No.	Item	No.
looms	12	spinning wheels	81
spindles	4	cards	23
combs	2	windles	5
heckles	12	brake	1
creels	3	warps	2
gig wheel	1	fulling mills	3
shears	9	shearboard	1
tenters	2	presses	3
teasles	2	dyes	1

From a Sample of 628 Inventories, 1558–1700, in Lancashire Record
Office. (For Area, see map p. 21.)

Raw materials: wool and fibre

Sheep

Altogether 228 inventories (36% of the sample) showed holdings of sheep.
To gauge the amount of wool these animals produced, the period 1550 to
1700 was divided into two blocks, pre- and post-1600. In each period the
average price per sheep was calculated using those inventories where
number of sheep and value was noted. This average price was then used
to calculate the number of sheep in the inventories where just a value was
given. Twenty-five inventories listing sheep were ambiguous, so they have
been omitted leaving a sample of 203 testators holding a quantifiable
number of sheep. This is clearly only a rough guide, as there has been no
attempt to separate sheep newly-sheared from those carrying a full fleece,
or sheep from lambs. The price of sheep seems to have risen considerably
in the seventeenth century but the figure for the latter period was influenced
by one particular holding where sheep were valued at 7s. 8d. each, which
was significantly higher and indicated that they still carried their fleece.
Tables 2.3 and 2.4 show the result. The holdings ranged from just one
sheep to 213 with only seven people owning over 100 animals.

TABLE 2.3 Holdings with sheep

period	Average holding of sheep	Average price per sheep	Average wool yield (lbs)
1550–1600	25	3s. 0d.	50
1600–1680	34	4s. 3d.	68
1550–1680	30	3s. 7d.	60

Range of holding was from 1 sheep to 213.

TABLE 2.4 Actual holdings from 203 inventories where sheep could be calculated

No of sheep	Holders	Percentage of sample (%)	Wool yield in stones
0–10	61	30	<1.5
11–50	106	52	1.5–7
51–100	29	14	7–14
101–200	5	3	14–28
Over 200	2	1	>28

Source: See Tables 2.1 and 2.2.

How long would it take to spin the wool from these animals? The likely amount of wool capable of being produced by these sheep was calculated using the values adopted by John Marshall, that is two lb. of fleece per sheep. Each household's wool holding was calculated solely from the amount of wool one could expect from the number of sheep kept, and *not* from any wool held in the inventories, which would have varied depending on the season the inventory was taken in, the time of clipping, and whether any of the wool stock had been sold. It is intended only to test whether there was enough wool being produced to indicate any large-scale woollen production in the Lune Valley. As shown in the table, one could expect about 60 lbs. (just under four stone) of wool from the 'average' flock kept. Using the standard measure for a woollen kersey, that is eighteen yards in length, one yard in width and two stone in weight, and allowing for some wastage, one could expect about forty yards of cloth from these four stones of wool. The average holding of cloth in the sample was just seven yards, perhaps the equivalent of a blanket and a skirt so it would appear to mean there was a surplus of thirty-four yards from each average holding which would be available for market. However, realistically the bottom 30% of households listed hardly had enough sheep's wool for their own needs and 64% would probably produce just enough for themselves, possibly with a small surplus, and only the top 4% had enough either to trade fleeces, perhaps to Kendal, or to act as small clothiers themselves, having the fleece spun locally, and maybe even woven up locally. Apart from the few large sheep holders, therefore, few households in the Lune Valley produced sufficient wool to cover the farming families' needs and generate a surplus that could be sold to the local non-sheep holding community or the local market.

Although it was not included in the survey of inventories, however, we know that Hornby Castle Estate was trading wool. The 1582 accounts show several references to the Lord's store of sheep, the receiving of tithe wool, the selling of tithe wool, payments made for the washing and clipping of the sheep, and one entry noting the receiving 'of Allan Carre for 108 st wool combing as well as the Lord Store as of the tithe wool stores sold to him at 9/- stone ... 58/14/0.' It is possible that he could have been buying for the Kendal woollen trade, which at that time was producing serges and bays, both using a worsted warp with woollen weft, or for the local hosiery trade, where worsted yarn would be more suitable than woollen yarn being smoother against the skin, and more hard wearing round the heels and toes. Whether these sheep were situated within the Lune Valley, however, is far from clear since the estate held extensive grazing land elsewhere in the region, most notably at Cotterdale in Wensleydale.[8]

Other fibres and yarns

Inventories also show holdings of fleece, raw hemp and flax, and of yarns of wool, hemp and flax. This was difficult to quantify accurately as inventories often listed several categories of yarn and fibres, but sometimes did not specify them individually. Two hundred and thirteen inventories (34% of the sample: Table 2.1) held some raw material or yarn. Sixty inventories listed yarn only; the remaining 153 contained 168 references to hemp, 75 to wool and 49 to linen. The average holdings, however, were low. Only one and a half stones of hemp and three stones of wool, and only one decedent, Robert Eskrigg of Eskrigg in 1670, showed signs of larger-scale production, having £8 worth of wool in store. He also had a flock of 186 worth £45. A significant point, however, is that 85 inventories referred to a specific fibre and yarn priced together, i.e., 'hemp and yarn 8s.' and, as these were often found amongst the household goods, it is reasonable to surmise that the change from fibre to yarn must indicate the presence of spinning. This will be dealt with later.

Of the 63 inventories specifying both yarn and price, the average holding overall was 9s. 0d., the smallest being 4d. the largest 30s. 0d. Francis Croft, the weaver (see below) held thirty leas of yarn worth 2s. 0d. The 30s. holding of 'Yarn hempe and flexe' was that of Thomas Curwen Esquire of Gisgarth, Caton 1589, and is the only indication of larger-scale production in the sample. Again, therefore, it would seem that raw materials, that is fleece and fibres, and the small individual holdings of yarn suggest nothing more than domestic activity in the Lune Valley, with the exception of a few larger producers or dealers.

Cloth production

Carding, combing and spinning

Further evidence of possible production, however, can be gleaned from holdings of tools and cloth. Carding and spinning were skills learnt at the mother's knee, first to be useful to the family, and second, for the girls, to gain a husband, or to supplement future income. There are many examples in contemporary literature, paintings and journals from the Middle Ages onwards which bear out the fact that from the poorest cottager, through minor gentry to royalty, women could spin.[9] However, in the Lune Valley sample (Table 2.2), there were just 23 cards, 2 combs, 4 spindles and 81 spinning wheels. How accurate a portrayal is this likely to be of domestic production?

The very small instances of combs is not surprising since combing was generally done by men, possibly working together away from the home. Combs were usually heated, perhaps to release the lanolin in the wool as it was drawn through the combs, thereby preventing the long fibres from breaking. There is a difference between this and carding wool which results in a rolag, where all the fibres lie horizontal to each other and have a spring-like elastic quality, and which, when spun, results in a soft yarn that gives when pulled. Combing wool, however, results in a sliver where the fibres lie vertical to each other; it produces a smooth, hard-wearing yarn with very little 'give' and a slight sheen, and is generally used to make worsted cloth. Long stapled fleece is necessary for this process. The reference to Allan Carre above suggests that a considerable amount of fleece was being combed somewhere, although precisely where is far from clear. This would have been a considerable task, and it is possible that it was done by a team of carders working for the Hornby Castle Estate since wool combing was an occupation which demanded great skill. Lipson considered that

> The most striking feature in the condition of the wool-combers was their itinerant character. No class of workmen appears to have attained more nearly the economist's ideal of mobile labour, for they were accustomed to travel about the country from place to place in search of employment ... and when work was scarce in their native town, they were not compelled to accept low wages in order to save themselves from starvation.[10]

If this was the case in this area, then it is *possible* that itinerant woolcombers, possibly from Kendal, may have routinely travelled through the Lune Valley picking up work, and that could account for the lack of combs as inventory evidence.

It is difficult, however, to take the low figures for cards and spinning equipment at face value. In the first place, there are less than half the number of cards as there are spinning wheels, and yet every spinner would have carded her fleece. Not to do so would have resulted in a yarn so

Woman Spinning. A print depicting of domestic spinning and carding in Yorkshire, 1814 (From George Walker, *The Costume of Yorkshire*)

uneven and lumpy as to be unusable, unless the fleece was of exceptionally fine quality and the spinner very skilful. Spinning was an essential skill for women of all social classes. Wadsworth and Mann considered that 'Carding and spinning ... were the most widespread of industrial occupations – a spare-time occupation of most women of the industrial and agricultural classes ... As a by-occupation spinning prevailed far outside the weaving districts.' [11] Even better-off women would spin in their parlours. Sarah Fell and her sisters at Swarthmoor Hall, for example, spun wool on their imported Saxony wheels whilst employing the local women to spin the hemp and flax on their great wheels.[12] Spinning was also an early form of welfare. In the Quaker community, women's meetings allocated fleece to their less fortunate sisters, allowing them to pay for the wool as they sold the yarn.'Also this day returned to our meeting by the hands of Sarah Fell from Agnes Holme of Hawkshead a poor woman, four shillings and sixpence which was lent her (out of stock) in 7th month 1676 to buy her some wool with to keep her in employment'.[13] Wool, hemp and spinning wheels were also given out to help keep the poor off parish relief. In the industrial areas of intensive production, where fleece was delivered to the spinners, it may already have been carded but in a rural area with little other evidence of large-scale commercial organisation, this seems unlikely. There is however, nothing to rule out the possibility that if there were several children in an overburdened household, they may have been encouraged to card fleece for others in the community, to add to the family's income. There are even fewer heckles, which would be just as essential to the hemp and linen spinners.

Only six spinning wheels were listed prior to 1600. The reason for this is puzzling. Primitive spindle spinning may still have been common amongst the poorer people and it is known that spindles and whorls were still being produced at Forton in 1687. But spinning wheels had been in use since the Middle Ages, and by this period it is likely most women would be using them, with the spindle used as her portable work tool, whether in the fields whilst flock watching, or perhaps when socialising with other women in the village.[14]

In addition to inventories with spinning wheels, however, a further 85 listed fibre *and* yarn together, in 55 cases amongst the other household goods such tables and chairs. How did this transformation from fibre to yarn take place without a spinning wheel? Even with the comparatively low level of sheep-holding evident in the inventories, it would have taken 35 women to spin all the fleeces, working full-time, at an accepted rate of spinning of half a stone in a six day week. Research on the Furness district, however, showed that the women only engaged in spinning from Autumn through to early Spring; the rest of the year they were working in the fields, planting hemp seed, weeding, muck spreading, hay-making etc ... We can probably assume that Lune Valley women would be doing the same, nearly doubling the number of women needed. This estimate ex-cludes the considerable amount of spinning that must have been done for Hornby Castle, although against this it is possible that some of the large wool growers included in the sample may have sold their fleeces outside the district unspun. Flax and hemp spinning might account for as many again, not only of women spinning for their own harden and sacking, but for the canvas and sail making industry in Lancaster. A realistic estimate, therefore, might be nearer 200 spinners active at some time in any one year.

Logistically, therefore, the low numbers of spinning wheels and carding equipment in the inventories are just not feasible. The answer to the conundrum may lie in the nature of the equipment and in prevailing attitudes towards its ownership by those undertaking the inventories. Carding equipment was small and primitive and needed to be replaced regularly. A spindle was very small and may well have been included in the general term 'husslements'. These inventories also show that common great wheels were not expensive – around 8*d*. to 1s. 0*d*. where they were valued separately – but generally they were bracketed together with other goods as though not worthy of separate mention.

Furthermore, if we look at the 73 inventories which were taken for female decedents we get more clues as to why spinning equipment might rarely have been mentioned. Of these, ten listed a spinning wheel of which seven were women with a flock of sheep and other animals suggesting they were farming on their own behalf, as widows or daughters, and that the appraised goods belonged to them in their own right and were considered to be used for commercial purposes. For example, among the items which Isabel Dobson of Caton, widow, left in 1642, were old sheep and lambs, wheat, hemp and beans, wool and broken wool (carded), cards and a spinning wheel. The other three spinning wheels were left by women with very few other personal possessions. In these cases it is possible to surmise that the reference was there for a particular reason. The wheel which belonged to Elizabeth Burrow of Arkholme (1676), was not listed in her inventory with the 2s. 0d. worth of yarn, but in her will, where she bequeathed 'to Agnes Lambertson my woolwheel', suggesting that she had been spinning up to her death but had ensured the wheel went to a particular person. A further twelve women kept sheep and animals. The smallest holding belonged to Margaret Edmundson of Caton (1577), who had sheep worth 4s. 0d.; the other eleven left flocks ranging in value from 13s. 0d. to £1 8s. Such women with stock and husbandry gear appeared to be in charge of the farm at the time of their death, and maybe had family living with them, where perhaps daughters were spinning, so the wheel was not shown in the testatrix's inventory. The remaining women without spinning wheels or animals but with fibre *and* yarn were presumably spinning but their equipment was not considered sufficiently important to mention.

What seems likely, therefore, is that where a woman actively engaged in husbandry and had family living with her, and had yarn listed in the inventory but no wheel, the wheel could have passed unremarked to the next female. Where a woman, whether living alone or independently engaged in husbandry had no natural successor, the wheel was listed in the inventory or was bequeathed separately in the will.

There may be other reasons, related to men's different roles, why wheels do not appear in male inventories. We can speculate that if a wheel was found with odd lumber, then it was likely that the decedent was a widower or an unmarried son, and the wheel not in use at that time had no natural successor, and that where a wheel was listed with yarn and cards, it was obviously in use and the appraisers had counted the wheel as the decedent's possession. But it is highly likely that, where the existence of yarn and fibre indicates that there was spinning activity, but no wheel was listed, it was the case that the appraisers considered the equipment as morally, if not legally, belonging to the bereaved female, as it may well have been essential to her future ability to provide for herself. It would be interesting to know what social considerations the 'four honest men' took when they were at their appraising.

Weaving

It is also possible that weaving looms did not appear in inventories because they had already been taken over by natural successors since even clearly identified weavers did not always have looms listed among their possessions. Only twelve individuals in the sample listed looms, and two of those, Alexander Bankes of Austwick (1592) and Francis Croft of Lancaster (Scotforth) 1680, were slightly out of the main survey area.

1558   John Banke of Tatham
1567   John Gybson of Melling
1592   Alexander Bankes of Austwick

1616   Robert Claughton of Leck
1622   Anthony Dickinson of Gressingham
1623   John Hewetson of Burrow
1649   Edward Chippendell of Claughton
1662   Thomas Dowthwayte of Newton
1671   Edward Dickinson of Whittington
1673   Thomas Townson of Caton
1678   Robert Padgett of Caton
1680   Francis Croft of Scotforth

The extra information in the inventories reveal little about these men. Most appeared to be engaged in husbandry with the studdles, stoodles or looms and work tools, as they were described, being mentioned almost incidentally. The most detailed was that of John Banke of Tatham 1558 who left 'heckyll ... wole ... creels £5 15s. 7d.' and 'studyls with healds and reeds 4s. 0d.' together with 'quilt quishon webb of 12 yds; blanket webb of 12yds.'. Francis Croft left 'two p[ai]r of weaver looms and all the gear belonging to the trade of a weaver £1 18s. 0d.' plus 8d. worth of woollen yarn and 30 leas of linen worth 2s. The disparity in the price of John Banke's looms and gear and Francis Croft's two looms and gear is possibly accounted for by the 120 year gap between them, although the degree to which appraisers always correctly valued goods is unknown. Thomas Townson of Moorside, Caton (1673) was described as a shearsman but his inventory listed no shears or other work tools. His will, however, stated, 'I give unto my said son [Thomas] all the worke looms and tooles belonging to our trade except one paire of great sheares which I used myselfe which I give unto John Townson my young son'. This last example, however, must be treated with caution, as the original meaning of 'loom' given in the Oxford English Dictionary was simply the implement or tool one worked with. He may not have been a weaver.

The low number of weavers in the sample, however, may arise from the fact that, although some weavers made a respectable living, especially if they had more than one loom working and were able to weave more complicated cloths, in general weaving was a poor trade, and those involved in it were less likely to leave wills than other craftsmen or those with land and stock. If this is true, then we have again to look to other sources for other clues to get a truer picture of the extent of weaving activity.

The probate records themselves provide some indicators. William Bracken of Hornby described himself in 1694 as a linen webster in his will, but he did not bequeath working tools, nor was there an inventory. He did not appear to have immediate family, for his bequests were to nephews, and his executor was James Bland, husband to Margaret Bracken, daughter of another William Bracken, a yeoman of Hornby. But this indicates some weaving in the Bracken family, and an earlier Bracken, Robert in 1637, had left 'sacks with some canvas yarn' and 'one canvas webb'. This web may have been prepared to take to a weaver, but it may be that Robert Bracken had it ready to go on his own loom.[15] Another Bracken, William of Scotforth, left 'a gig wheel and working tools' in 1672.

Other references to weavers occur in schedules of debts taken from inventories such as John Berry's of Caton (1638) which referred to debts owing to John Rippon of Caton, webster. The inventory of Gabriel Croft of Tongmoor, Littledale (1636) showed obligation charges to Robert Croft in Caton, webster, and that of Henry Croft of Claughton (1641) showed 10 yards of cloth added to his inventory after it had been totalled, possibly because the cloth had been with a weaver at the time the inventory was taken. There may also have been a connection between these Crofts and the weaver Francis Croft mentioned above, as the names Francis, Henry and Gabriel occur frequently in one branch of this large family, and Francis Croft's own brothers were christened Henry and Gabriel. Francis Croft is also particularly interesting, in that he could be the weaver employed by Sarah Fell of Swarthmoor Hall to weave two rugs for her mother Margaret Fox in 1673. Her wool was carried across the sands from Ulverston to Lancaster by Higgins, the Swarthmoor carrier, where it was woven into the rugs by Croft and collected three weeks later, again by Higgins, and taken back to Swarthmoor. This long-distance commission was carried out even though Sarah Fell had her regular weaver living within a mile of Swarthmoor.[16]

Another weaver appears in the inventory of John Chambers, shoemaker of Caton (1583), where we find 'item that Robert Weringe webster doth owe him to be paid 13s. 4d. in hand and 13s. 4d. at Candlemas and 11s. 8d. the first whole weeke of lente ... 38s. 4d.', and another in the will of William Parkinson of Hornby, schoolmaster (1664) where land is left to his son 'situate and being in Hornby which I bought of William Claughton of Hornby aforesaid, webster'.

Parish registers also suggest rather more activity. Those for Caton show that a Robert Hodgson, webster, had children christened between 1626 and 1633, but although there are ten Hodgson inventories in Caton between 1616 and 1674, including one Robert who died 1669, there is no indication of any one of them weaving. Another source, the Quarter Session Rolls, lists John Battie of Burrow as a webster in 1605, but again, despite the large numbers of Battys in the probate records there was no indication of weaving, although one might expect that the trade would have been carried on in the family.[17] Finally, the Hornby Castle Estate accounts for 1581–2 note the following: 'Also paid by the said Thomas Marshe for spinning wool and hemp for the lady's use 11/-. And to the webster for weaving the cloth maid of the said hemp 4/4. And for expenses of Elizabeth Baytson going to the webster for to warp the web 4d.'.[18] This item raises a matter which I will discuss in the next section, but for the moment we can take it as one more example of a weaver.

Despite this small increase in the number of identified weavers, however, references are scattered over a long period (1558–1684) so one can only conclude that local weaving at this time was, with the odd possible exception, for the local market, the distribution of weavers reflecting the demands of that community. It was probably the custom in rural areas for the yarn to be taken to the weaver already warped, or as illustrated above, someone may have been paid to go and make the warp for the weaver, who then charged a rate per yard for weaving the cloth. It is unlikely in this limited domestic system that weavers speculated by buying yarn to weave up to sell to an outside market. Weaving was possibly a part-time occupation, taking place when attention to crops or animals allowed. The people involved might well have fallen into the section of the community that did not often leave testatory evidence, accounting for the limited references in probate records of the trade. It is certainly the case, from personal research elsewhere, that even when there was a loom specified in the documents, the testator, if in a will, or the decedent, if in an inventory, was described as a husbandman or even a labourer rather than a weaver.

Warping

Of all the processes involved in the early textile industry, warping is the most elusive. No account of the history of textile production seems to cover this activity fully. Herbert Heaton, who gives the most detailed account of the whole process from sheep clipping to the production of saleable cloth, only explains the process from when the 'yarn is brought home'. He goes on to say 'that part of it which was intended for the warp had to be spread out, wound to the back "beam" or roller, placed in the loom, threaded through the healds or heddles … and finally … fastened to the front beam'.[19] He does not comment on how the warps were made, nor more interestingly by whom they were made. The Kenyon Manuscript on the 'Techniques of Yorkshire Woollen Industry' c. 1588 lists 'instruments' but does not mention any warping gear, nor does warping appear in the description of the distribution of labour.[20] Furthermore, in the early inventories taken in recognised centres of handloom weaving, such as around Prestwich and Oldham, where looms are frequently found in the cottages, it is rare to find references to warping walls (woughs, wolles), together with the looms, even though much smaller items of equipment such as cards are listed. Warping equipment was more often found in the inventories of clothiers or chapmen who were in the business of handing out warps and who made them on their own premises.[21]

Early warping equipment was very basic, needing only four pegs rammed into the ground or more conveniently into a wall. Three pegs formed the cross, which was necessary to stop the threads getting tangled, and the fourth determined the length of the warp (see opposite). The disadvantage of this was that with a long warp, the warper had to walk a considerable distance, and a refinement was for the pegs to be set in a sturdy wooden frame, so the warper could zig-zag the yarn round the pegs from a standing position. The frame could be any size and the peg arrangement could vary apart from the cross pegs (which later appeared at the end as well as the beginning of the warp), the whole being either free standing or fixed to a wall. It is likely that this frame is what is meant by the term 'warping wall', which appears in inventories in the sixteenth and seventeenth centuries. (see below)

It is surprising that this activity, which after all comprises half of the finished cloth, and is a tedious, time-consuming and tricky business, has been so overlooked in this early period. The logistics of turning hundreds of spinning wheel bobbins holding two to three ounces of spun yarn into a large 'skein' containing anything from eighty to several hundred 'ends', possibly up to thirty-six yards long, and getting them to the loom untangled, are not inconsiderable. Winding the larger bobbins from small spinning wheel bobbins required equipment, as did the warping itself, which involved drawing continuous threads from bobbins held on a creel so they could run freely, and winding them round a series of pegs, putting in a cross to ensure the threads remained in the order they were warped, to whatever length and width was required. The more ends warped at once the quicker the process was, but it was very slow, and it required a certain deftness. When the warp was completed, the cross was tied securely, the warp chained off the frame, and it was then completely transportable.

Who, then made the warps which were produced for local domestic use? It is unlikely that the weaver did. For one thing, warping equipment does not appear often enough in inventories, although it could have come under the all embracing term 'weaving tools', or, as pegs in the wall, been regarded as part of the structure of the building. For another, the time

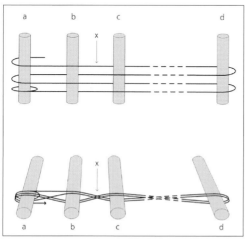

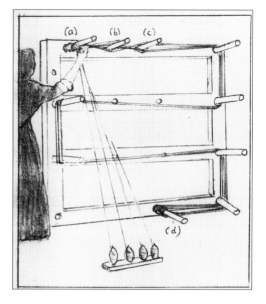

Warping pegs showing the formation of the cross. The distance of peg (d) from the cross defines the length of the warp.
Warping Frame (*right*)

taken to make a warp by hand was (and still is) considerable, and rates of pay for weaving, at one and a half pence to three pence a yard, make no allowance of pay for warping. Lastly it is the sort of work that was traditionally carried out by women, another reason which may account for its low profile.[22]

This is why the above references to webs (warps) in inventories, and that of Elizabeth Baytson (see above) going to make the warp for the weaver are of interest. As already mentioned, in this early domestic textile industry it seemed usual for the spun yarn to be provided by the local people for the weaver to weave. Perhaps it was also their responsibility to do the laborious warping up themselves by using the simple method of pegs hammered into a wall or stuck in the ground, if they did not possess a warping frame. Samuel Bamford, writing of south Lancashire at the end of the eighteenth century, observed that after the women had finished their household work they engaged in spinning the wool and forming it into warps for the loom. Maybe, too, the weaver allowed the women to warp their yarn on his warping equipment for a small charge since Elizabeth Baytson was paid expenses for going to make the warp for the weaver, or maybe somewhere in the community was a communal warping frame for general use. Without evidence of warping equipment, however, we cannot know, except to say that this process must have been carried out somewhere in the district.

Fulling and finishing

The survey of Hornby Castle Estate in 1581–2 mentions a fulling mill in Wray, one part holder being Thomas Proctor, and one disused mill in Hornby Park. The survey of probate records produced three more men in Caton, each in possession of a fulling mill, or part of a fulling mill. Indeed all of the finishing equipment listed in Table 2.2 was found in Caton except for two shears, which by their context were probably for shearing sheep rather than cropping cloth.

In 1630 Barnaby Carter of Caton willed to his son Barnaby Carter 'the woolle meole w[itlh all that belongeth to the occupationnes as tenter and shearer and all other things thereunto apper-taninge to the said occupation'. Five years later in 1635 the inventory of Henry Carter listed shears for his trade, and he willed 'all my sheares tenters and whatever work tools I have belonging to my trade to my brother James Carter', whose own inventory in 1638 listed tenters and tenter wood, shears, a press and other implements. His will, however, did not bequeath any of this work gear nor, as with Henry, was there any mention of the fulling mill, originally bequeathed by Barnaby.

In 1628 Geoffrey Stovin's inventory listed a pair of cloth shears, a press for cloth and teasles. In 1677, Geoffrey, grandson of the above Geoffrey, bequeathed to his father, Edmund, a shearman, 'all my p[ar]te and porcon of my fulling mill scituate in caton aforesaid together with shears and other ... belonging to the said mill'. His inventory listed one pair of shears, one scythe and one axe.

The third fuller was Robert Parkinson of Brookhouse, Caton. His inventory of 1667 listed tenters, shears, shearboard and a press, and his will bequeathed 'his messuage and tenement at Brookhouse ... and likewise the fuller milne ... unto his son John' and 'all the tenters shears and implements belonging to the said milne'.

From this, we appear to have three fullers operating in Caton from 1628 to 1677. This might seem to indicate the presence of a reasonable cloth-finishing trade which extended beyond the local domestic production. But is this the case?

First, let us define 'fuller' as being the man *in possession* of all or part of a fulling mill. It needed capital outlay to provide the mill race, and fulling stocks, but the act of fulling needed no special skill, the cloth was put in the trough with water and fuller's earth, and the stocks were then allowed to pound the cloth to shrink and thicken it. Judgement was needed to determine how long the cloth was worked, but the main complaint was that the cloth was deliberately removed from the mill too soon, in order to make it appear longer. In the sixteenth century many Acts were passed to prevent the fraudulent stretching of cloth which would shrink the first time it got wet. J. May in his *The True Estate of Clothing in the Realm* (1613) commented on the practice: 'in our owne countrie where much of our wool may be vented, the falsehood of clothing is so common that every one striveth to wear anything rather than cloth. If a gentleman make a liverie for his man, in the first showre of raine it may fit his Page for Bignesse!'.[23]

In the main cloth-producing areas, the fuller appeared to be occupied with this one process, passing the cloth on to other skilled men or back to the clothier, for nap-raising and shearing. The sheer volume of cloth to be processed would make this single operation viable. In the Lune valley, however, there seemed to be less specialisation. The fullers also carried out the more skilled work of tentering, nap raising, and cropping and they passed on the tools to their heirs, referring to them as the tools of their trade. The fulling mills, however, did not, according to the probate records, always get passed on with the rest of the estate.

It is also possible that there were not three mills. Let us take the case of the Stovin and the Carter families. Their dates are parallel, both families are engaged in tentering and shearing, and both families possessed part of a fulling mill at some time. Are these two mills, or could it be we are looking at just one? When Geoffrey Stovin died in 1628, he left a nuncupative will, in which he asked that his tenement be left to his wife (with the usual provisos against her remarrying) until his son Edmund came of age. Edmund then had to pay certain sums of money to his sisters. No mention was made of any tools of the trade, but they were listed in the inventory, as we have seen. One of the two people described by Geoffrey

Stovin in this as his very good friends, and asked to hear his last wishes and to see them carried out, was Barnaby Carter. Barnaby Carter died two years later, leaving a fulling mill to his heirs. When they died within the next eight years, the fulling mill did not appear in their inventories or wills, and they appeared to leave no sons. In 1677 when Geoffrey Stovin, grandson to the above Geoffrey, died he left his part of a fulling mill to his father, Edmund, a shearman. It is possible to conjecture, therefore, that Barnaby Carter, in possession of the mill in 1630, had shared the business, or employed Geoffrey Stovin the elder, and as the Carter family had died out part of the mill had been taken over by the younger Geoffrey Stovin which he left to his father, Edmund. In fact, Edmund Stovin who was contemporary with Barnaby Carter's sons, may have already had a part of the mill, which he had shared with his son Geoffrey.

Shared ownership is also evident in the Parkinson family who held part of a mill in 1667 which continued in the family until after 1709/10 when Francis Parkinson of Caton appeared as a fuller in the Rolls of the Freemen of Lancaster.[24] When he died unmarried, he left his brother Richard 'the Messuage Barn and Stable ... and likewise one half of the Fulling Mill and a Close called Walkmill Parrock containing about one rood as also all the Tenters Shears and any other Implements of a fullers Business thereto belonging'.[25] We know where this mill was, but not who owned the other half.

This information raises difficult questions. Did fulling mills change hands as owners died or leases came to an end, leaving the skilled shearmen to carry on their trade, either working for the new owner/tenant of the mill or by tentering and finishing cloth brought to them by people who had taken their cloth to the fulling mill, maybe paying for the use of the fulling stocks? What is the significance of Caton? Obviously it had the water power, but so had other places in the Lune Valley, and yet of the seven fullers listed in the Rolls of the Freemen of Lancaster between 1709 and 1762, all bar one of those in the locality were at Caton. (The other was at Ellel.)

Interestingly, in addition to Francis Parkinson, the five remaining Caton fullers listed in the Rolls were made up of two families who followed on from each other, again a possible indication of only the existence of just one mill.

It is difficult to know precisely who these local fulling mills undertook work for. Possibly the proximity of Hornby Castle and other large houses was significant, with their need for blankets, for cloth to clothe servants and estate workers, and other textile requirements. Work may, of course, have been drawn in from a larger area. James Carter (1638) was owed 3s. 0d. by William Scott of Ingleton for cloth cropping. It is possible that cloth might have been brought from Lancaster, but Lancaster weavers also wove linen, and hemp for canvas sail cloths, which were not fulled. Whether they dealt with ordinary cottagers is even less clear. If they were spinning their own yarn, and taking it to the weaver to be woven up, did they take their piece of cloth to the fuller, perhaps some distance away to be finished? Or did they do what had been done in the past, and was still being done in Scotland even into this century, that is, putting the cloth in a tub of hot water, with urine, and treading it themselves until fully shrunken and thickened, then stretching it on a roller or stretching it out behind the house to dry?[26] Significantly only one possible dyer was found in all the probate inventories, that of William Armetstead of Gressingham (1615), who had listed 'one copper pan and some part of loadel (lid?) joined to it for dying 18s.' and he had a 25s. debt 'to one merchant of Yorke for stuffe'.

The finished article – cloth

With one exception cloth holdings suggest that they were for domestic use. In the 41 inventories which specified the type of cloth, there were harden, hemp, linen, linen tow, sack cloth, canvas cloth, white cloth, white kersey, woollen cloth and two happins, all locally produced cloths. There is one reference to 'mesline' possibly muslin and 'mellow' cloth (unknown) which may have been bought at Lancaster. Research in the Furness district has shown that, although cloths such as set out above were locally produced, better quality cloths such as Scotch cloth, Yorkshire cloth, silks etc. were bought at Ulverston market, Kendal or Lancaster. The happins (coverlets) are of interest in that this is a term used often in Swarthmoor accounts where Sarah Fell employed spinners specifically to spin happin warp. It was measured in leas so was of linen, but it is not known whether the weft was also linen or whether it was wool since the term was one which would appear to have only been in use locally. Where yardage was specified in 19 inventories the average quantity was just seven and a half yards, the exception being the inventory of William Bordrigg the elder, yeoman of Whittington (1661) which listed 'new cloth £6 10s. 0d.' which could be have translated to upwards of 100 yards. His total assets were valued at £428 and he may well be a rare example of someone acting as a buyer.

Conclusion

Although there is little to suggest that people in the Lune Valley engaged in significant textile production during this period, there is sufficient evidence to suggest that they probably engaged in enough activity to keep themselves in basic textiles. They had access to raw materials, carded the wool and spun the yarns in their homes, made the warp or had it made, then took it to the weaver, who wove up the cloth charging by the yard for work done. The cloth was taken to a local fuller and then sheared before probably being stored by the owner until it was needed to be used for hard wearing working clothes and aprons, warm capes and tunics, shifts, bed linen, blankets and coverlets, mattress ticking, sacks and window-cloths and possibly shrouds. Services were possibly exchanged and skills bartered throughout the community to provide for this domestic need, and large-scale commercial activity had to wait until the coming of the water-powered mills towards the second half of the eighteenth century.

The difficulty in trying to assess the extent and organisation of textile production in the Lune Valley during this early period, however, remains the lack of detailed evidence. We are dealing in the main with common people, and they left no records to speak of, except at death. A lot of assumptions have to be made but, as J. F. C. Harrison has written, 'if we start by asking the right questions and looking for answers in new directions we may at least stand the chance of uncovering more than has been discovered about the common people in the past. The starting point must be those things which were central in the life of labouring people.' [27] Textiles were surely that.

Notes

My grateful thanks go to Emmeline Garnett, who drove me all round the area and gave me invaluable information gleaned whilst researching her book on datestones, and to the Search Room staff of the Lancashire Record Office for their speedy production of the Probate Documents which have provided the bulk of the evidence for this chapter. In view of their large number, I have chosen not reference each one of them separately, but readers interested in specific individuals should be able to locate the relevant documents from the information provided in the text. All general comments on the processes involved in cloth production are based on the writer's own experience as a handloom weaver and any opinions are her own.

1. A. P. Wadsworth & J. de L. Mann, *The Cotton Trade and Industrial Lancashire, 1600–1760* (Manchester University Press, 1931), chapter 1; J. T. Swain, *Industry before the Industrial Revolution; North East Lancashire 1500–1640* (Chetham Society, Third Series, Vol. 32, 1986); N. Lowe, *The Lancashire Textile Industry in the Sixteenth Century* (Chetham Society, 3rd. Series, Vol. 20, 1972); E. Roberts (ed.), *A History of Linen in the North West* (CNWRS, Lancaster University, 1998).
2. W. H. Chippindall (ed.), *A Survey and Year's Account of the Estates of Hornby Castle, Lancashire* (Chetham Society, New Series, Vol. 102, 1939).
3. Swain, *Industry*, pp. 128–9; M. Brigg, 'The Forest of Pendle in the Seventeenth Century', *HSLC.* Vol. 113, 1961; J. D. Marshall, 'Kendal 1661–1801: The Growth of the Modern Town', *TCWAAS*, New Series Vol. 75, 1975.
4. Swain, *Industry*, p. 129; B. Pidcock, 'The Spinners and Weavers of Swarthmoor Hall, Ulverston in the late Seventeenth Century,' *TCWAAS*, Vol. 95, 1995.
5. J. Nicolson and R. Burn, *The History and Antiquities of the Counties of Westmoreland and Cumberland*, Vol. 1 (1777), p. 11.
6. F. Eden, *The State of the Poor* (1797), pp. 554–5.
7. A photocopy of her unpublished reminiscences is in the Lancaster Library Reference Library. I am grateful to Emmeline Garnett for this information, and for the dates of the Miss Turners referred to, who were born between 1741 and 1761.
8. Chippindall, *Hornby Estate Survey*, p. 101.
9. E. Lipson, *The Economic History of England: Vol. I, The Middle Ages* (10th edition, Adam & Charles Black, 1949), p. 443: 'in Anglo-Saxon times the mother

of King Alfred is represented as skilled in spinning wool and the chronicler Fabyan relates that Edward the Elder "sette his sonnes to score and his daughters he sette to woll werke"' Fabyan, *The New Chronicles of England and France* (1811 edition), p. 176.

10. Lipson, *Economic History, Vol. II, The Age of Mercantilism*, p. 52, citing House of Commons Journal, Vol. XLIX, pp. 323–4.

11. Wadsworth & Mann, *Cotton Industry*, p. 274.

12. Sarah Fell bought a 'Dutch Spinning Wheel' from her married sister which she gave to her unmarried sister, paying 10s. 0d. for it. This was probably what is known more often as a Saxony or Brunswick wheel, an advanced type where the wheel was turned by a foot treadle, so freeing both hands for the drawing out of the thread. It also had a 'flyer' which allowed the continuous winding of the yarn on to the bobbin whilst spinning was taking place. The simpler great wheel used by local women cost between 8d. and 2s. 0d.

13. Cumbria Record Office (Barrow), Quaker Women's Monthly Meeting Minute Books, 1671–1700, BDFC/2 Box 5–8: 4th day 7th month 1677. Olwen Hufton, *The Prospect Before Her: a History of Women in Western Europe Vol. 1, 1500–1800* (Harper Collins, 1995), p. 327 quotes from London Magdalen home for prostitutes, set up in 1758, where women were put to work 'to make their own cloaths, both linen and woolen, to knit stockings from the new materials, spinning the thread and making the cloth.'

14. D. Winterbotham, 'Early Linen Manufacture in the Manchester Region', in E. Roberts (ed.), *A History of Linen in the North West* (CNWRS, Lancaster University, 1998), p. 28.

15. It has been pointed out that the Oxford English Dictionary's primary definition of web is 'A woven fabric, spec. a whole piece of cloth in process of being woven or after it comes from the loom.' It is not necessarily a warp. If, however, one takes examples of the word being used in context, it is generally used in the meaning of a warp, or a structure in the process of being woven. For example, '1797 Encycl. Brit. (ed 3) xviii 835/2. The breast bar, a smooth square beam in which there is an opening to let the web through as it is wove.' and poetically – '1820 W. lrving, Sketch Book. A Royal Poet 1.171 "That passionate and fanciful armour, which has woven into the web of his story the magical hues of poetry and fiction"'. It would seem safe to read web as warp, or as in Scotland, the cloth newly cut from the loom and still unfinished, but it is obviously open to question.

16. Pidcock, 'Swarthmoor'. There appears to be only one Francis Croft in Lancaster at this time, so it is assumed he is the same weaver as used by Sarah Fell. The two rugs woven by Francis Croft could have been the 36 yard length of cloth known as a rug. This would mean he was paid 2d.–3d. per yard for weaving them. Although described as a linen webster, there is no reason why he should not also have woven wool.

17. J. Tait (ed.), *Lancashire Quarter Sessions Records* (Chetham Society, New Series, Vol. 77 1917), p. 277.

18. Chippindall, *Hornby Estate Survey*, p. 118.

19. H. Heaton, *The Yorkshire Woollen and Worsted Industry* (Oxford, 1920), p. 109.

20. R. H. Tawney & E. Power (eds), *Tudor Economic Documents Vol. 1, Agriculture & Industry* (Longman, 1924), p. 216 – 'Three score persons are thus to be divided: 12 for sorteinge, dressings and lyttinge the woolle, 30 for spinninge and cardinge; 12 for weaving and shearing; the odd 6 persons to heipe the reste as go to the miline and tourle etc'.

21. Lowe, *Lancashire Textile Industry*, p. 20.

22. For example in F. Thompson, *Harris Tweed: The Story of a Hebridean Industry* (David & Charles, 1969): 'in the days when Harris Tweed was in its infancy and was little more than a cottage industry producing for home consumption only, the warping was done with only two threads, so that it took almost two days to warp a length of tweed. The warping was originally done by women.' See also D. Defoe, *A Tour Through the Whole Island of Great Britain* (Yale U.P. reprint, 1991), p. 121 shows a plate of women winding and warping for the weaver taken from the *Universal Magazine of Knowledge and Pleasure*, Vol. 5, October 1749.

23. Heaton, *Yorkshire Woollen Industry*, pp. 124–44.

24. 'Rolls of the Freemen of the Borough of Lancaster 1688–1840', *Record Society of Lancashire and Cheshire*, Part. 1, A-L, Part II, M-Z, vols 87 & 90 (1935 & 1938).

25. E. Garnett, *The Dated Buildings of South Lonsdale* (CNWRS, University of Lancaster, 1994), p. 45.

26. Thompson, *Harris Tweed*, pp. 46–56.

27. J. F. C. Harrison, *The Common People: A History from the Norman Conquest to the Present* (Fontana, 1984), p. 14.

CHAPTER THREE

Quarrying and Extractive Industries

Phil Hudson

The history of quarrying, clay and shale extraction in the Lune Valley probably dates back to the time when man first colonised the area immediately after the ice of the last glaciation retreated, and the population began to fashion stone tools, weapons and quernstones, and use clay deposits to make crude pottery. Random stone picking for burial mounds occurred in the hilly areas such as Yorkshire's Three Peaks and up on the limestones of the Lune's upper reaches, but there is little evidence to suggest any quarrying as such associated with this activity. Firm archaeological evidence of what might be termed 'industrial' exploitation of primary resources dates to the Romano-British period. Some two thousand years ago the local indigenous population appear to have used certain types of gritstone for quern and millstone making and local clay to make pottery. The Romans carried on this exploitation and developed pottery and tile making kilns in Quernmore, a few miles east of Lancaster.[1] More evidence of primary resource utilisation comes to light during the medieval period when pottery is known to have been manufactured on several sites.[2] This was also a time when much more use was made of stone for building but, like most early industry in the Lune Valley, the surviving archives contain very little information until the fourteenth century. Reconstructing the history of quarrying and extraction, therefore, has to rely heavily on the interpretation of the landscape and archaeological evidence. This chapter draws primarily on the author's primary research into the development of sites in the lower Lune Valley, broadly defined as running from Lancaster to the lower slopes of Ingleton but also incorporating Hutton Roof, Bentham and Mewith.

Stone: walls, flags and slates

The landscape evidence for previous quarrying manifests itself today as holes, hollows, and disturbed ground. Unlike coalmining sites, which are very localised, these are ubiquitous. Almost every farm, common, upland moorland or fell area has evidence of man's exploitation of material in the solid and drift geology. The reason for this widespread practice is simple; most stone was not usually carried very far from its quarry source. Old quarry holes and abandoned larger quarries (if not named these are often called Town Quarries on early maps) are thus a common feature in the Lune Valley landscape and most of the stone that was extracted from these was used locally in field walls and drains, general building and road metalling.

However, there are within the solid geology of the Limestones, Silurians and Namurian Grits, places where the different grades and types of rock provide a medium which has special qualities and uses. Some grits are of millstone-quality,[3] and there are the cherts, found in certain limestones, used to make tools in the Neolithic and later periods. Other types have proved valuable resources for roofing slates, flags, columns, quoins, lintels, gatestoops, stone troughs, cheese presses, roadstone and good-quality building stone. In the post-Conquest and later periods stone was also increasingly quarried as special building materials for urban use such as ashlar facing or for church building, decorative sculpture or columns, or increasingly for slates for roofing and flags for paving. These products were often moved some distance from their source. However, it is not until the early seventeenth century that all types of stone are brought into regular use for building work. This survey concentrates on some of the more important sites which have been identified, providing site references for readers who may wish to inspect them.

Lancaster, Quernmore and Caton

In the lower reaches of the Lune, near Lancaster, some of the ganisteroid massives and gritstone beds have been used for cut stones. Field research has located several areas on Caton Moor where there are the remains of large horse troughs, stone water tanks, gatestoops, and lintels. Quoins and material for similar objects have also been quarried from the rocks on Black Fell, Claughton Moor, Littlefell and Otter Gear, and millstones were cut on Baines Crag and from most of the readily available high quality gritstone beds.[4] (Map 3.1). Rough slates were taken from Birk Bank and Caton Fell, and finer slates from the Littledale quarries. Ashlar facings came from Black Bank, Caton Moor and Birk Bank, while columns and other high quality massives were to be found at Mainstones and Welby Cragg.

It is not easy to date when this quarried material was first taken into the town of Lancaster. Some was certainly used to build the castle and the priory church in the immediate post-Conquest period and the town was allowed a 'Paviage Grant' in 1340.[5] From this date flags, cobbles and setts (small cut blocks of stone) could have been laid in the streets. A survey of surviving stones in several areas in the town found quite a mixture of stone types in street kerbs and pavings. Some stretches have mixes of Ganisteriod, some unknown and both Black Fell and Birk Bank types. Back streets with setts have an even wider mixture of types which include some millstone-quality stone, while the early cobbled areas have mixes of local grits, water-washed river-bed types and glacial erratics.

Much of the 'town stone' used to re-build Georgian Lancaster during its
'Golden Age', relied on local stone taken from the quarries on Lancaster
Moor and Common (now part of Williamsons Park).[6] The pace of building
was such that the diarist Stout recorded in 1739 that he had difficulty in
finding masons to complete a house he himself was erecting in the
town.[7] Arthur Young described the town in 1770 as 'built of white stone
and slate',[8] and it was also aptly observed and recorded by Christopher
Clark in 1807 as a stone '. . . that was soft when quarried but became surface
hardened on exposure to air, so it was much sought after',[9] especially the
types which were free from iron-stain seams and which came from Knotts
and Lancaster Moor Quarries. John Holt, writing in 1795, also noted that
'Near Lancaster (upon the common) is an extensive quarry of excellent
free-stone, which admits of a fine polish. The county town (Lancaster) is
built wholly of this stone, and, for its neatness, is excelled by few towns in
the kingdom.'[10] Other named quarry sites which were used by the town
are at Wallers, Greaves, Denny Beck and Pointer. Most of the old Lancaster
quarries, however, were given up by tenants by 1809 due to a fall-off in
demand for building stone and were not re-opened until the revival of
housebuilding in the last quarter of the nineteenth century.

Outside the town's extents the vernacular-styled farmhouses, barns and
cottages, many of which date from the rebuilding of mid-to-late seventeenth century, have door lintels, frequently carved with the initials of the
lessees or owners,[11] and quoins made from the harder local grits or
ganisteroid rocks. Thin beds of these ganisteriods have been quarried at
Littlefell and Cow Close, possibly in association with some coal-mining as
at, for example, Rough Lot and in adjoining Gibson Wood. The late
eighteenth-century Quernmore Park Hall (designed by Harrison), the later
Escowbeck House at Caton, and subsequent Victorian buildings in Lancaster and improvements to Gresgarth Hall, as well as many other fine
Lune Valley houses have 'ashlar facings', pediments, porticoes and massive
columns, all in stone cut from selected local quarries. The stone for
Quernmore Park Hall almost certainly came from Knotts Quarry.

In the field boundary walls in the Lune Valley, however, it is possible
to see a very wide date-range of local stone of various qualities including
water-worn and field clearance stone (in use as walling stone, for gateposts,
stoops and styles). A large number of small quarry holes, stone/slate delves
have been recorded and mapped, and it is assumed that these workings
would have been used by the farmers and landowners to extract bedrock
for building walls and hedge banks, and in some cases for random freestone
for house walls and other buildings. Many of these small field quarries
probably date from the late eighteenth or early nineteenth century, and
were exploited particularly for walling the commons and Parliamentary
Enclosure Award fields. Others may have had more recent use as sources
of freestone or roadstone.

There are a few exceptions where high quality walling stone was sent

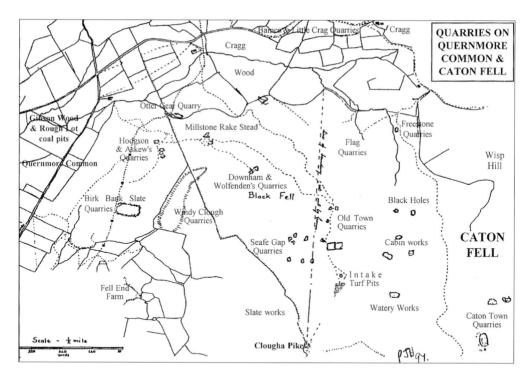

QUARRIES ON QUERNMORE COMMON & CATON FELL

Map drawn by Phil Hudson.

some distance. On Lancaster Moor and Quernmore, for example, there are sites which were brought into use in the twelfth to fifteenth centuries to provide building stones for Lancaster, and there is evidence that the right to stone was considered a privilege and was well regulated. A 1362 list of Constitutions and Orders for the town of Lancaster (No. 138) states that, 'Noe man shall take his neighbours' stones, being in the quarries'.[12] These quarries were also used for walling stones for some of this period's major enclosures, such as deer parks, vaccary lands and the expansion of the Gresgarth-Hollinhead estate in the late fifteenth century. But generally the stone for wall fences was never carted very far, so that the availability of outcropping, easily-quarried stone determined the types of fences set up at the time.

Stone slates have been won in the lower Lune Valley area since the medieval period and the right to mine or get stone and slates appears to date from this time. In the Lancaster area, this right was possibly part of the privileges granted by Count John in 1194.[13] Only one reference has been found to date, contained in a Rent of Assize return of 1440, which states that there was no income that year from the slate quarries in Quernmore, indicating that these had been worked and yielded income in previous years.[14] Unfortunately the location of the place name 'Spatongill', a slate quarry site named in the document of 1440, has not survived, but it is assumed that the site was a gill in Quernmore where there is an outcrop of the type of rock which can be worked to produce a reasonable roofing slate.

It is not until the seventeenth century, however, that there was an upsurge in the working of the slates in the Lune Valley. This was done mainly to provide roofing material for the newly-built or extended stone houses and buildings in the area and subsequently in Lancaster. As early as 1635 Lord Morley of Hornby Castle, Master Forester of Quernmore, complained about the behaviour of the people of Lancaster in the Forest of Quernmore who were 'taking away many cart loads of coal, freestone, slate and spoiling the ground for livestock by digging great holes and pits.'[15] Lord Morley appeared to have been at a loss as to how to stem the tide of these activities and works demanded by the seemingly ever-increasing needs of the local population for these resources from the forest hinterland. It would seem, however, that the Lancaster men had quarry rights from ancient times, as mentioned above, while other sites were also leased out.[16]

Buildings in the Quernmore area often have roofs of Birk Bank slates, most of which date from before the later half of the seventeenth century. A fine example of changes in local stone used to extend buildings is the now ruinous Fell End Farm (SD 533 599 but on private land). Lancaster Library has an old photograph of it when it was still occupied and intact. This shows the 1660 and 1720 building phases and intact roofs. The 1660 dated buildings were roofed with rough 'Birk Bank Flags', taken from quarries nearby, while the 1720 dated buildings had been roofed with the finer 'Littledale Slates'. These latter quarries are known to have been opened up after the turn of the eighteenth century. The sources of roofing slate from the forest area, however, cover many sites found on Birk Bank, Black Fell and Caton Moor. The main named sites are known as Birk Bank, Black Hole, Cabin Works, Seafe Gap, Watery Works and Old Town. Intermixed there are several unnamed sites spread over several square miles of the moorland and fell.[17]

There are just two documents and an early map which survive for the historical record of these. The first document was a lease of 15 years dated 1714/15, granted by the Lord of the Manor of Caton, Edward Riddell, to one Charles Leah of Quernmore, showing a rent of £3.15s, allowing him to win slates on Black Fell in Caton.[18] The lease included supply on demand by the Lord of two roods of dressed slates at any three times during the term of this lease. The second document is an indenture dated 1738 between the Mayor, Bailiffs and Commonality of Lancaster, and Robert Parker, John Caton, and James Leigh of Quernmore, husbandman, for the seven-year lease of a slate delf.[19] This lease gave them the right to delve '... slate or flags ... from the bottom of Birk Bank Scar all above that scar ... to the top of Clougha, within the liberties of Lancaster ...', for a yearly rent of £2 10s. 0d. to be paid in equal amounts at the feast days of Easter and St Michael (September). This lease had an unusual clause which gave the men of Lancaster some priority to any slates so they should not be deprived of supplies by the lessees selling to outsiders. The price was also controlled, with Lancaster men to pay only 'such prices as are usual'.[20] This appears to have been a right which was considered important, possibly exploited as a traditional part-time rural industry, and again is strong evidence that forest slate and flags were a valuable resource to the Lancaster townspeople. The map is dated about 1800 and marks most of the quarries mentioned above.[21] This map also gives some names of the quarry lessees, including a section of quarry worked by Hodgson & Askew, about halfway up Millstone Rake on Birk Bank (SD 545 608). Hodgson & Askew also worked Seafe Gap Quarry (SD 543 603) up on Black Fell. Another site between Conder Head and Little Windy Clough (around SD 545 603) was worked by Downham and Wolfenden.[22]

There are problems with trying to date precisely the periods during which most stone quarries operated. Even though many are presumed to be of ancient date most of those located along the line of the Thirlmere water pipeline, which was laid in the late 1880s, were reopened and used to provide stone for the lining and other works. The same can be said for quarries adjoining works connected to the building of the canal and later the railways. These, together with the need for walling stone after the eighteenth and nineteenth-century enclosures, has removed most of the clues that could be used to interpret ancient workings. Although the Mainstones-Damasgill quarry (SD 519 565) was later worked for the Thirlmere aqueduct stone, when some 91,000 cubic yards of stone was removed,[23] it has already been established that it is of ancient date with a long period of use.[24] The quarry was used to provide a special type of stone for buildings in Lancaster during the eighteenth century and White notes that 'the stone from Damasgill seems to have been selected for special purposes. We can only assume that it was specified because of particular characteristics, such as resistance to water, or the availability of long lengths without flaws.'[25] In 1762 the monolithic columns for the Lancaster Customs House were cut from Damasgill stone, as were the columns for the eighteenth-century Town Hall, and the stone for the New Quay at Glasson Dock, built in 1787, also came from Mainstones. There is no doubt that Mainstones, with its high-quality stone, would have been an important quarry, perhaps the most important in the area, possibly much earlier than before the well-documented eighteenth-century use. It is odd, therefore, that the research for this chapter, like that of White, finds no reference to it on Yates' Map of Lancashire of 1786.[26]

Hutton Roof

Hutton Roof had a series of working quarries producing millstones as early as the thirteenth century.[27] From the late eighteenth to early twentieth century, it became an important quarrying area; in fact most of the economy of the township was based on quarrying and mining, quarries here yielding grindstones, flags and building stone.[28] Named sites, mostly dating from the eighteenth century, are Longfield (High and Low); Brown Bank; Croft Ends; Hutton Roof Flag and Grindstone; Jacks Wood,

High Head; Moss Lots; Atkinson's; Bownasse's, North's and Park Limestone, with associated sites at Docker Moor, Whittington, Sadler Nook and Sellet Hall.

Weak manorial control and absentee landlords from the late fifteen century meant that quarrying and coal mining developed concurrently with agriculture, leading to an open type of community, characterised by religious non-conformity, self-governing village organisations and dual occupations.[29] Even after enclosure in 1822, which in many areas usually meant the death of free quarrying, the main quarry still belonged to the village and thus was in great demand for field walling stone. As Hyelman states, 'it bolstered the economy of the community and possibly the seed which laid the foundations of the development of the flag, grindstone quarrying and mining that quite quickly became the township's major industry'.[30] These quarries, in contrast to most others in the study area, which were often worked as part of the dual-economy, appear to have been well-financed and mechanised, initially possibly from kinship networks, but later on through prominent quarry owners. A lease of 1835, for example, has a windmill on one site (upper township quarry) for pumping equipment. The lower quarries also had steam pumping equipment, but these were given up in 1880 due to the high cost of pumping and excess water, and the upper ones were reopened using the transferred steam pumps.[31] Possible families involved in both coal and stone working in the area were the Holmes (local pre-1765), Huck,(?), Dent (from Burnley) and Atkinson (from Lindale) who all held land as farmers. George Atkinson, born *c.* 1771, who owned Moor End Farm, worked the township grindstone quarry as a share and bought land on the Moor on enclosure from the commissioners about 1820. He also sank a coalpit and set himself up as 'Contractor, Quarry and Colliery Master'. He also leased Docker Moor Quarry in Whittington, and laid a railway line to move out products. Grindstone makers and quarrymen who have been identified include the Bownass, Berry and Wearing families and, later in the nineteenth century, the Clarksons of Carnforth.

Hornby Castle Estate quarrying records

Hornby Castle Estate operated or supervised the getting of all types of stone within its Lordship and there seems no doubt that, as the nineteenth century wore on, its quarries grew in importance and became a regular source of revenue as well as providing local employment. It is also possible that the estate bought from other sites. The estate's archives contain quite a number of named stone-working sites including Backsbottom, Banespark, Hornby Park, Nutgill, Melling, the Town's Quarry in Hamskill Gill, Bentham Moor Lot, Jones Bank, Fearnsides Quarry at Backsbottom, Lower Kellet, Wilson's Quarry at Backsbottom, Mr Wright's Quarry, and Wegber Quarry. Local township quarries were usually worked for rough stone by the local populace for general walling and the highway surveyors for road-making stone, the latter probably being waste material from the quarries' other products.

Backsbottom Quarry, in Roeburndale above Wray, was an important source of stone, particularly slates. This was run by the Ripley family on a lease from the Hornby Castle Estate for many years. It was probably opened up in the early seventeenth century since many of the houses of this date in Wray have slate roofs from this quarry. Backsbottom is particularly well documented for the early nineteenth century, when the Hornby Castle Estate used it as a source of good quality slates and flags. These were set out and worked in ridds. The account books show that the Ripleys, or named persons, were either hired directly or extracted ridds by agreement with the estate manager who made regular visits to take stock.[32] Some of the quarrymen in this area were migrants from the Rossendale area. The site has no buildings extant, only relict foundations can be seen, one of which was possibly a base for lifting gear and a steam-powered crane site with coal and boiler clinker heap, an old track-way washed out by the river in places, and a walled cutting to the south. The stone here is a mix of massive bedded grits, thin roofing slate and thick bedded flags. Backsbottom, and some other minor local sites in the area working the same fine-bedded gritstone beds nearby, were the only local source of good roofing material available until the railways began to bring in lightweight Welsh and Cumbrian roofing slate, although there is

Backsbottom Bridge, Roeburndale, c. 1900: This carried a track along which horse drawn vehicles could bring down stone from the quarries. Both the bridge and a farm just up river from it were swept away in the flood of 1967. Neither was rebuilt and woodland now obscures many of the old workings. However, it is just possible to distinguish the remains of trackways and earthworks associated with the stone slate quarries. (*Lancaster City Museums*)

evidence of some slate being brought into the Lonsdale area by coastal shipping, and later via the canal. Slates and flags from Backsbottom were carted as far as Lancaster and Heysham to be used as roofing and flooring material.[33]

Banespark, near Hornby village, was used to get good quality stone for estate building work. Wegber, and some beds in Backsbottom, had massive bedded strata which was used to cut gatestoops, lintels and doorheads. The stone beds in Hornby Park Quarry were of good quality and had several uses. Stone was taken from it to build the new Loyne Bridge over the Lune at Hornby in 1815. When the turnpike road was being altered and improved the Commissioners ordered new milestones from it. The event is recorded in the estate records: 'Sept 6th 1821: Told John Turner in what part of Hornby Park Quarry he was get stones for milestones'. Ashlar facings were also cut as on 11 January 1822: 'Mr Wright getting stones in Hornby Park by Robert Jennings at 2d per square foot for ashlar'. In the same year Robert Unsworth had permission to cut new stones for the repairs to Wennington Bridge. In 1825 the demand for stone from this quarry was such that the estate installed a crane. This was not removed until 2 April 1828 when George Smith and Enoch Knowles with some estate labourers moved it to a new working area at Backsbottom.

Nutgill Quarry in Ingleton township was mainly worked for its good quality flags. It is known to have been worked for sandstone slate before the 1767 Bentham Moor Enclosure since it is marked as such on the boundary maps. James Berry and Thomas Charnley are often mentioned in the estate records in connection with this site. The quality of the stone was such that when building works were being carried out at Hornby Castle flags were specially ordered and carted the seven or so miles. 'July 30th 1821, Henry Towers brought a cartfull of Flags from Nutgill Quarry for the Hall Floor' ... 'Sept 2nd 1821, Bank's 4 carts and our 4 carts fetched flags from Nutgill for flueing the further hothouse.' On 11 June 1830 George Smith records, 'I then went to Nutgill Quarry and ordered a rood of 2nd slate from William Thompson for £3.6.0.'

Earlier, in 1819, when Bentham Moor was being further enclosed, several quarries were used as a source of walling stone, and for stone tiles to be used for land drains.[34] The Bentham Moor Quarry was still being worked for these purposes in 1844 to wall George Wright's allotment there. The estate also sold stone to the locals and jobbing contractors from this site. 'Sat July 10th 1824: Richard Ray of Mewith called about buying stones from Bentham Lot Quarry', and 'April 1st 1824: A Mr Wood called about getting stones in Mr Wright's allotment on Bentham Moor for building a bridge over the Greta on the line of the new diversion of the Kendal and Keighley Turnpike Road.' When Overend extended Bentham Mill he bought the stone from Hornby Estate's other quarry in Low Bentham. 'Thur Jan 19th 1826: Mr Overend of Bentham Mill called about getting stones in Jones Bank Quarry'.

Ingleton district

Further up the Lune Valley, other sites were becoming more important, particularly the sites that had stone with special qualities. In Ingleton township blue slates were worked to produce flags and roofing material.[35] The so-called 'Ingleton Granite' was valued for road-metalling.[36] Further afield in Dentdale, 'Dent Marble', a hard crinoidal limestone that could be polished, became fashionable for making floor coverings, decorative columns and fire surrounds.

Ingleton slate quarries were short lived. Hutton refers to them in 1780 with some praise as '. . . fine large blue slate affording useful and ornamental cover'.[37] They were found in a thin bed, possibly part of the Cambrian Greywacke inlyer, which ran north/south for up to two miles, and 200 to 300 metres wide, on the north bank of the River Twiss, with the main quarry located near Thornton Force. The sites were worked intermittently from the mid-eighteenth century, but never on a large scale and they were either worked out or uneconomical by 1860 when the railway brought in quantities of cheaper Welsh and Lakeland slate into the area. The last owner-operator was George Coward, who is assumed to have worked 'Greens' in Quarry Wood on the east bank of the River Doe (SD 703 742). The slate was in local demand for roofing, flagging, making water tanks, cattle boskins and still-room tables but, according to Hewitson in 1885, it was not considered to be very good export quality.[38] In the valley sides of the Twiss and Doe, there are extensive remains to be seen today, including the faces of the ridds, features which could be filled shafts where the product was mined rather that worked in open ridds, and a lot of waste and spoil.

The other major site is one that exploited a non-limestone rock, the so-called 'Ingleton Granite'. This was in Chapel-le-Dale, on the north side of the Low Sleights Road (SD 718 753). Here is a bed of Greywacke inlyer, Ordovician period metamorphic pyroclastic impervious sedimentary grits and slates, quite different from the blue slates worked in the valleys of the Rivers Doe and Twiss. It is unique, almost vertically bedded, has a greenish colour made up of quartz grains with feldspar, mica and secondary chlorites, and is not found anywhere else in the Ingletonian Series. Its commercial value is in its high crushing strength – some 43,000 pounds per square inch – which makes it ideal for use as road-metalling stone.

The history of its discovery and initial exploitation is a classic example of late Victorian entrepreneurial business.[39] This stone was first located by Adam Sedgwick during his Geological Survey of the area, and quickly investigated by one John Scott, railway contractor from Darlington. He bought the royalty and rights to extract on the site in 1886–7, and developed and worked it until March 1895.[40] On the dissolution of the firm, the works were then sold to R. J. Dent of Leeds, one of the partners, for £7000, although it seems that Scott stayed on, perhaps as manager, for he was granted an explosives license in 1902.[41]

Ingleton Granite
Quarries, *c.* 1909
(Phil Hudson,
adapted from 1909
25 inch OS map)

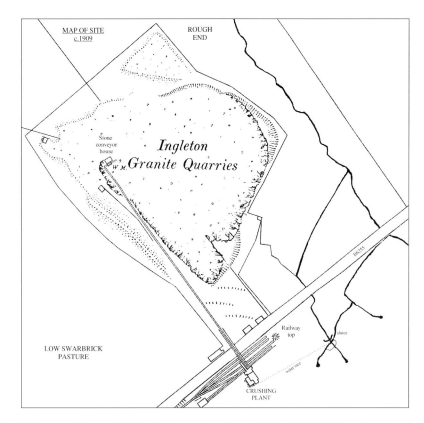

Ingleton Granite Quarries, c. 1900. The quarry buildings and incline plane are both clearly visible. Note the horse drawn waggons in the foreground. This method of bringing stone from the quarry floor survived almost till the site closed. (Phil Hudson collection)

The quarry was on the north side of the road, where the main body of this rock deposit is found, but the quarry works, with the screening and crushing plants, were on the south-east side of the road. The quarried rock was carted on a horse drawn flat-bed in the quarry bottom. The trucks were then hitched on to a cable drum to be hauled up the steep gradient on a ramp and a gantry over the road to the main quarry buildings. A tramway took the crushed stone to the sidings at Ingleton Station. The tramway was built in the 1880s by John Hewitson, engineer and contractor of Ingleton, and the local press reported that it gave work to many unemployed villagers who were thrown out of work by the closure of the colliery.[42] This tramway was standard railway gauge and in two sections. The first section was pulled by horses and later, once the bed had been reinforced, by a steam locomotive. It ran on a flat bed, on a gradient of approximately 1 in 70 from the quarry buildings on a line parallel to the Low Sleights Road following the 800 ft. contour, veering away from the road by Skirwith to the south-east, crossing Fell Lane to end at the Winding Drum Top (SD 709 728). The second section that moved the stone down to the station sidings was straight laid single track, with a single cross-over point crossing under the old Ingleton-Clapham coach road (SD 703 726) and lower down, over Jenkin Beck by a bridge (SD 701 725). It worked on a gravity feed on a 1 in 6 gradient, with the weight of loaded trucks pulling up the empties. Later, in about 1924, this gravity feed system, and the rail flat-bed, was replaced by an aerial ropeway set on 26 towers, ranging from 10ft. to 72ft. high, that took all the quarried material in buckets straight from the quarry site to the railway sidings at Ingleton station. This system was used until after the Second World War, when it was replaced by road

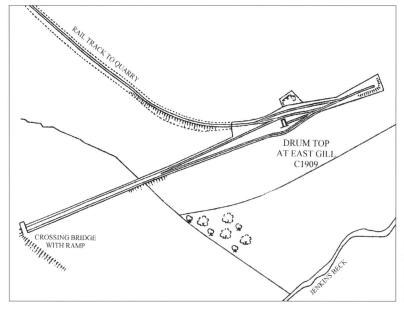

Drum Top, Ingleton Granite Quarries c. 1909 (Phil Hudson, adapted from 1909 25 inch OS map)

lorries. This quarry is now closed, and very little evidence remains today, apart from the huge hole in the ground, a ruined building on the crusher site, and fragments of the flat rail bed, bridge abutments, bases for the drum-heads, and some of the concrete bases for the ropeway towers. The owners, however, are still working the same 'granite' bed at Skirwith.

More extensive workings in the Ingleton area rely on the various grades of limestone which is crushed and burned for both agricultural and industrial use.[43]

Ingleton 'Granite' Ropeway Tower with Tom Wilson. Constructed about 1924, this aerial ropeway took quarried stone in buckets from the site to the railway sidings at Ingleton station. This system was used until after the Second World War, when it was replaced by road lorries. (Phil Hudson collection)

Limestone: agriculture and industry

Lune Valley limestone, wherever it outcropped, has been worked by local farmers to supply their own field lime-burning kilns especially since the early eighteenth century.[44] Evidence for early use of limestone for local farm use can be seen in the almost ubiquitous lime-kilns which are dotted around the limestone uplands. Almost every large farm had one of these to provide burnt lime for its own land. The residue was often sold to local smallholders and farmers whose land lacked carboniferous limestone rock. Limestone had long been important in the agricultural economy.[45] It was burnt in kilns, usually in close proximity to the quarry site. Some of the early examples are the 'sod' or 'field' types which lacked a stone-built structure. These produced slaked lime to spread on acid soils to improve fertility. Extensive use for lime burning was made of the limestone at Kellett and Ingleton. Once the railways were built, however, a new market outside the immediate environs of the kiln sites emerged for this product and led to the commercial expansion of some of the established sites and the setting up of new kilns elsewhere.

The first example of commercial lime-burning kilns was at Kellet in the early nineteenth century when a kiln and quarry site were rented from Hornby Castle Estate. The sites do not seem to have been very profitable, for the Hornby records often mention the estate manager, George Smith, pursuing long overdue bills for coal sent to the kilns from the Hornby-Tatham pits. However, the Hornby Estate also had kiln sites at Ingleton which were operated in the early nineteenth century by John Walling, limeburner of Moorgarth (and possibly one Gamaliel Briscoe) who also apparently contracted to deliver and spread his products. George Smith's diary regularly records such instances: 'Fri Dec 3rd 1819 Mr Wright agreed with John Walling to lime part of Hornby Park at 13 and a half pr(sic) per load'; 'Sat Jan 23rd 1820 John Walling of Ingleton called about payments for Lime and was desired to call again'; 'Fri January 28th 1820 Mr Wright paid John Walling's son £40 on account for Lime'; 'Fri July 21st 1820 Thomas Blezard and I went to Kellet to order some lime of Henry Miller for Over Salter building'; 'May 21st 1822 Thos Towns from Kellet called about midday for a lime kiln there'; 'June 9th I and John Hoyle went in the morning to the New Lime Kiln at Kellet Ends Lane near Low Kellet, which James Alexandra and sons had built and were finished off today'; 'Wed June 22nd 1822 Went to Kellet and measured the flugh (flue) done there by Towers and Woodhouse for a Lime Kiln'. In 1825 there was also a kiln operated by William Armitstead at Wennington, on the Green, which must have been working limestone brought in from quarries several miles away.

This industry continued to be controlled by Hornby Castle well into the nineteenth century and all the evidence suggests that it continued to expand. The accounts show that the kilns were usually operated on a rental

Hoffman Lime Kiln c. 1900. The horses and carts waiting would have been used to take processed lime to railheads or directly to local customers. (Courtesy of Bill Mitchell)

or lease basis, and several names appear as 'burners' to whom accounts were paid and bills sent for the coal used in the kilns. 'Feb 20th 1839 I received £10 a year's rent of Quarry at Lower Kellet from the Mr Edwin Sharp'. 'March 10th 1842. I met James Alexandra at Kellet End Lane near Low Kellet when we examined the situation as to building a Lime Kiln'.

The earliest recorded limekilns at Ingleton appear to be selling kilns, although there were ones operated part-time by farmers and commoners on Storrs Common and Mealbank. There was only one limeburner, William Tomlinson, recorded in the township in 1803.[46] The remains of a double kiln can still be seen on Storrs (SD 701 735) and the area is pocketed with small quarry workings, trackways and other remains. However, the earliest remains on this site have been disturbed by mid-nineteenth-century workings when limestone was extensively worked commercially by Robinson of Skipton who built large kilns (SD 699 735) and employed the locals to get the limestone to burn in them. Robinson's activities also closed or altered the earliest of the riverside kilns, probably those that were worked in 1819–20 by the Wallings and by Joseph and William Preston in 1832.[47] By 1860 these kilns were rented by Robinson who expanded the works by building new kilns and ore crushers. The crushing of limestone was new to the area because the previous kilns had only been burning limestone to produce 'cob', the burnt stone which was transported whole to customers who 'slaked' it themselves. Robinson also used the railway to transport large quantities of crushed limestone rock to all types of customers and his innovative, but commercially unsuccessful 'limedust' to farmers. The site today shows the remains of the three kilns, associated grinding and crushing buildings, ramps and other works some of which remained in use until the 1940s (SD 699 734).

The main expansion of limestone quarries was across the river on the

Mealbank site (SD 695 735). This industry expanded from about 1855, after the railway had been brought into the area, to meet the demand for high grade lime for the chemical and steel industry, because bulk transport to these new markets was feasible. The business began to expand after Wilson and Clark, who also operated kilns on Giggleswick Scar, took over the lease of the kiln and quarry at Mealbank, possibly with a third partner named Thistlethwaite.[48] The demand for their high purity lime from industry was such that in 1868 it is thought they built a 'Hoffman' type kiln, having obtained a right to the patent. In 1872 they formed a new partnership with Charlesworth and Shepherd forming The Craven Lime Co. This new expanded company operated either from the enlarged, or possibly a new Hoffman Kiln with 18 chambers and 13 coke and coal feeding holes that was opened in 1873. Working on a continuous system, this kiln produced about 60 tons of lime per day.[49] However, the company had problems with carting their output up to the LNWR station at Thornton, about half a mile away, all of which was done by horse and cart. As a result, they began the construction of a mineral line from the Thornton sidings to their main works area on the west bank of the river in 1892, the remains of which can still be seen. Completed in 1895, this doubled their output and led to increasing prosperity for the village.[50]

Clay and shale: pottery, tiles and bricks

Substantial clay and shale deposits occur in Lunesdale and these have been worked on several sites. The Romans exploited the pockets of fine clay

Clay Drift, Waterside Pottery, Burton (above)
Blunging Clay, Bridge End Pottery, Burton (opposite)
The hard manual labour involved in collecting and preparing the raw material for production is clearly evident in these photographs, taken in the closing years of the potteries' existence. (*Lancaster City Museums*/Henry Bateson)

deposits in Quernmore to make pottery and tiles. There are several recorded in the medieval period, including one at Ellel which could date from *c.* 1200.[51] Many more recent sites are known, including an eighteenth-century pottery site at Newlands and another in the Lancaster Town area.[52] Local clay was also used to supply the Scotforth pottery in the nineteenth century.[53]

Burton in Lonsdale was a major centre of pottery production which flourished from the eighteenth to the twentieth centuries.[54] Over this period it is estimated that there were 15 pottery sites, but only scant remains of these can be found today. They all used to extract their clay and shale from abundant local deposits and used locally-mined coal to fire the kilns.[55] The Bentham Moor Enclosure Award of 1767 designated a six acre plot for the use of Burton potters, 'to be used by the owners of lands ... within the township of Burton aforesaid, for getting of clay, for the making of pots and other purposes ...' This site is thought to be around SD 649 716. Most pottery sites outside the confines of the village also had a clay or shale pit nearby, some had their own coal pits, others may have cut turf and peat for kiln firing. Most were family-run 'pot-shops' with just the one kiln, and a few workers, mainly producing earthenwares known as brown, white and black wares for local markets.[56] Later, after 1830, fireclay deposits found in the local coal seams were used to produce stoneware. The only evidence seen today is uneven ground and small hollows on the clay-shale extraction sites, often mixed in with the coal mining remains.

Small-scale brick kilns are recorded in and around Lancaster on the Lune (c. 1860–1912), Marsh (c. 1858–1900) and Glasson Brickworks (1864–1940), but very little evidence survives for these sites.[57] One, in Quernmore, a private company run by the Quernmore Park Estate, made rough bricks and agricultural drainage tiles, initially for the estate use, but also sold to local buyers. It was set up by William Garnett of Quernmore Park just after he bought the estate around 1850, but it was short lived and is thought to have closed by 1867. The census of 1851 does not list any workers there, and there is only one tilemaker listed in 1861. The site is now occupied by Tilery Cottages and there are no remains of the works, only grassed-over clay pits and puddling sites in the hillside above.

There are several examples of small brickworks being attached to coal-mining enterprises, making use of the seat earth clay found next to the coal seams and the mined coal for heating the brick-kilns. Two are in the Ingleton area, one operated by Bracewell at Wilson Wood and another at Barker's Enter Pit. The *Lancaster Guardian* of 16 May 1896 reported that Barker's bricks were in such demand that to meet it he had changed over from hand-made to machine-made bricks. There was also a works adjoining the coal pits in Burton in Lonsdale (SD 655 719), possibly run by Thomas Hodgson.[58] One other small works for which there is some information, and still evidence on the site, is on Bentham Moor (SD 701 693). This was recorded under various titles, generally as New Butts but also recorded as Chesters Tile Works.[59] The owners appear to have made both hand-made common bricks and drainage tiles from the late nineteenth century. The census for 1881 lists Stephen Parker, drain tile-maker at the Butts, with three workers. The site was probably abandoned in the 1940s.

However, the most recently developed clay and shale working has been for common brick and tile making. Clay and shale extraction in Lunesdale for commercial brick-making appears to date from the mid-nineteenth century, possibly influenced by improved railway access since before this date there is scant evidence of any large-scale commercial working. There was a site in Littledale (SD 563 631), owned by the Brookhouse Brick Co, that once made quality bricks from the local shale. The latter is thought to have worked from the early 1920s to the late 1960s. The site was cleared about 1980 and a new house built on it; all that remains are the extensive shale-pit workings and spoil seen on either side of Crossgill Beck.

The only commercial site which is still in use is located at Claughton, now trading as Hanson Brick. There were two main Claughton works, the earlier was called the Lunesdale Brick and Tube Co. of Caton, and the later one was often referred to as 'Claughton Manor', occupying sites either side of the present main road from Caton to Hornby. The earlier site was started by Thomas Baynes, yeoman farmer of Hole House Farm, Caton Green, who opened up land on a lease to LBT Co. to extract shale in 1874. Baynes held a fifth of the shares, until the company bought him out for £2000 in 1886, and also the freehold of the land from the Thorntons for a further £2000. The company expanded its operations and amalgamated with Claughton Brick Co. in 1897. The company brought clay and shale down from workings in Potters Hill Wood, via a tramway, parts of whose embankment still survive, to their works and kilns (SD 553 658). This site was closed by 1901, however, and the main works, by now called Claughton Manor, were on two sites further up on the other side of the Hornby road, known as West End (SD 559 661), opened in 1887, and East End (SD 563 664) opened in 1898. Both used to make tiles, but changed over to brick-making before 1900. The new works had sidings off the Midland Railway, and used shale dug from pits on Caton Moor (SD 577 648), brought down by aerial ropeways installed in *c.* 1900.[60] These ropeways are still operative today, providing the material for machine-extruded brick-making. Initially down-draft and Hoffman type kilns were used, but the last of these was demolished in 1982 when a new oil-fired plant was installed. The original ropeway bridges survive, though only the East End one is still in use, and several sections of the old brick-making buildings are still extant.

These works at Claughton and the Ingleton 'Granite' quarry are the only two nineteenth-century extractive industry sites still operational today. All the rest have gone out of business. Many of the sites have been cleared and levelled. Some have been put to other uses, others are lying derelict as relics of an industrial past, some, although in a ruinous state or almost buried, wait, hopefully, for historians and industrial archaeologists to explore and interpret them.

Notes

1. G. M. Leather, 'Excavations at Low Pleasant, Quernmore', *Contrebis*, Vol. I, 1972; G. M. Leather & P. V. Webster, 'The Quernmore Kilns', *Contrebis*, Vol. XIV, 1988; G. D. B. Jones & D. C. A. Shotter, 'Roman Lancaster: Rescue Archaeology in an Historic City 1970–75', *Brigantia Monograph*, 1988, pp. 85–93; P. J. Hudson, 'Notes on Roman Kiln Sites in Quernmore', *Contrebis*, Vol. XVIII, 1993, pp. 23–38. For a general overview of the pre-history of the middle Lune area see A. King, *Early Pennine Settlement* (Dalesman, 1970).

2. S. H. Penny, 'Pottery Sites at Newlands', *Contrebis*, Vol. VII, 1970, pp. 41–2.

3. P. J. Hudson, 'Old Mills, Gritstone Quarries and Millstone Making in the Forest of Lancaster'. *Contrebis*, Vol. XV, 1989, pp. 35–64.

4. P. J. Hudson, 'Millstone Making in Quernmore', *Lancashire History Quarterly*, Vol. 2, No. 4, December 1998 (published by Procter House, Kirkgate, Settle), p. 165.

5. Rev. R. Simpson, *The History and Antiquities of Lancaster* (Edmondson, Lancaster, 1852), p. 275.

6. A. White, *The Buildings of Georgian Lancaster* (CNWRS, Lancaster University, 1992); N. Dalziel, 'Trade and Transition, 1690–1815', in A. White (ed.), *A History of Lancaster, 1193–1993* (Keele University Press, 1993), pp. 91–144; D. Janes, *Lancaster, An Outline History* (Dalesman, 1980), pp. 32–46.

7. J. D. Marshall (ed.), *The Autobiography of William Stout of Lancaster, 1665–1752* (reprinted, Manchester University Press, 1967), p. 226.

8. A. Young, *A Six Months Tour Through the North of England* (1770), p. 196.

9. C. Clark, *An Historical and Descriptive Account of the Town of Lancaster* (Lancaster 1807), p. 65.

10. J. Holt, *A General View of the Agriculture of the County of Lancaster* (1795, reprinted David & Charles 1969), p. 12.

11. E. M. Garnett, *The Dated Buildings of South Lonsdale* (CNWRS Resource Paper, Lancaster University), 1994.

12. Quarries continued to be worked into the nineteenth century. Corporation revenue accounts show receipts from stone quarries of £67 14s. 0d. in 1831 and £50 9s. 10d. in 1851

13. PRO, Duchy of Lancaster Forest Proc. 29/17/1, m, 1d.

14. LRO, Rent of Assize; the accounts of Thomas Urswyk, master forester in

Quernmore from Michaelmas 1440 to same 1441; 'Quernmore of mines and millstones nil; of a mine of sclatston at Spatongill nil; from a mine of sclatston at Quernmore nil'.

15. LRO, Duchy of Lancaster Pleads, Chas 13, bdl 345.

16. LRO, RCHy. 2/2/34. A Lease dated 1661–69; lands in Lancaster to Johnson family, masons.

17. P. J. Hudson, 'Landscape and Economic Development of Quernmore Forest, Lancaster: An Upland Marginal Area in North West Lancashire, to *c.* 1850', Unpublished M.Phil thesis, Geography Department, University of Lancaster 1994.

18. LRO, DDGa 23 (2). Lease for 15 years at rent of £3 15s. 0d. from Edward Riddell (later Dalton) of Swinburn Castle, Co Northumberland Lord of the Manor of Caton, to Charles Leah (Lee) of Quernmore (Quarmore), Yeoman, a liberty to win slates upon Black Fell in Caton, dated 1 January 1714/5. These workings are outside the present Quernmore bounds in Caton Vill.

19. James Leah is thought to have lived at Askews or Humble Bee. He, and possibly his son, also James, are involved in the local affairs of the area, and the name Leah appears often in the local records.

20. Lancaster Reference Library, Local Collection, MS 1487.

21. Lancaster Reference Library, Maps Collection, PL 34/1.

22. P. J. Hudson, 'Old Mills'; see also R. Bellis & G. M. Shackleton, 'Slate Delfes in Quarmor', *Contrebis*, Vol. VIII, 1980, pp. 53–6.

23. LRO, Maps Collection, DDHH Box 35. A series of 7 maps with documents and correspondence dated 1886–9 show the survey for the pipeline works, with roads and quarry extraction plans. DDHH Box 4, 20 maps and documents, *c.* 1885–9, Mainstones and Welby Cragg Quarries with lists of charges, sections and quantities of stone extracted for Thirlmere contracts.

24. LRO, DDX 59/1 Map of Black House Farm, Ellel, proprietor Edward Weld Esq., by J. Sparrow dated 1774 shows a 'Mill Stone Field' (SD 520 570), north of 'Mainstones Quarry'.

25. A. J. White, 'Damasgill or Mainstones Quarry, Ellel', *Contrebis*, Vol. XIII, 1986–7, pp. 20–21.

26. W. Yates, *Map of Lancashire*, 1786.

27. P. J. Hudson, 'Old Mills'.

28. A. Hyelman, 'The Development of Quarrying in Rural Areas of Lonsdale and South Westmorland', Unpublished M.Sc. Thesis, University of Lancaster, 1984.

29. P. Gaskins, *Methodism in Hutton Roof* (1975).

30. Kendal RO, WD/Lons. In 1752 one unnamed family or group were recorded as arranging terms with the Lowthers for essaying a coal mine.

31. Hyelman, 'Quarrying', p. 242.

32. George Smith's Diaries (GSD hereafter), Vols 1–4, 1816–1859, Hornby Castle Muniments, 'Mon Nov 19th 1821 I went to Backsbottom Quarry to look at the completion of the rid by Edward Blezard and Co. Counted the gate posts got by them and took the stock of flags and slate on hand.' 'June 6th 1820 Richard Wilkinson called again about the soft flags at Backsbottom intended for the Hall, he is to begin cutting them tomorrow.'

33. GSD, 'Dec 26th 1820 Richard Grime called to see when the flags for the girls school at Lancaster, given by Mr Marsden, were to go.' 'Sat Oct 2nd 1824 Clifton and R. Gibson Jr went with 3 carts of slate to Heysham.'

34. GSD, 'Fri March 19th 1819 Henry Towers and 2 men from Bentham called about taking the draining of Titterington's Allotment on Bentham Moor.'

'April 5th, Mr Wright let the draining of the said allotments this morning to Christopher Jaques and Wm. Bowker of Burton in Lonsdale.' The average price paid for draining was 11*d.* per rood.

35. *Lancaster Gazette*, 31 March 1810. Advert for blue slate quarries at Ingleton 'to be let by private treaty'.

36. M. Humphries, 'The Development and Decline of Industry in the Ancient Parishes of Bentham and Thornton in Lonsdale in the Nineteenth Century', Unpublished Local History Diploma Dissertation, Liverpool University, 1984 (in Lancaster Univ. Library).

37. Rev. J. Hutton, *Tour to the Caves and Environs of Ingleborough and Settle* (1780).

38. A. Hewitson, *Guide & Visitors Handbook to Ingleton & District* (Preston Chronicle, 1885).

39. P. J. Hudson, 'The Ingleton Granite Quarry', *Yorkshire History Quarterly*, Vol. 5, No. 1, August 1999, pp. 41–4.

40. 1896 Return of Quarries under 1894 Act: Ingleton Granite Quarry: owner John Scott of Cotherston via Darlington; J. W. Tate manager; 27 inside workers and 17 outside. (John Goodchild collection, Wakefield Public Library)

41. *Craven Herald*, 29 March 1895; Humphries, 'Industry in Bentham and Thornton', p. 16.

42. *Craven Herald*, 2 October 1887.

43. Hutton, *Tour to the Caves*, 1780.

44. For information further up the Lune Valley see I. Cleasby, 'Limekilns and Limeburning in Sedbergh, Garsdale and Dent', *Sedbergh Local Historian*, Vol. 3 (3), 1994, pp. 2–10.

45. There is mention of a limekiln (limkulne) in Caton in the 13th century. See Cockersands Chartulary, Vol. III Part I, p. 832.

46. *The Craven Muster Roll, 1803* (North Yorks Record Office Publication, 1976).

47. White, *Directory of Lancashire*, 1838, Vol. II.

48. J. Carr, 'Recollections of Ingleton', *Lancaster Guardian*, 9 May 1896.

49. *Craven Herald & Pioneer*, 18 November 1892. This postulates that the Craven Lime Company was thinking of extending its kilns at Ingleton.

50. *Lancaster Gazette*, 9 May 1896.

51. A grant of land by Herbert of Ellel in *c.* 1200, names a potter's door and potter's pits in the boundary details, see Cockersand Chartulary. See also A. J. White, 'Medieval Pottery Kiln at Ellel, Lancashire', *Contrebis*, Vol. XVIII, 1993. pp. 5–18; B. J. N. Edwards, 'Late Medieval Pottery Kilns at Silverdale', *Contrebis*, Vol. II, No. 2, 1974, pp. 41–3; P. Gibbons, 'Docker Moor Medieval Pottery', *Contrebis* Vol. XII, 1985, pp. 41–6.

52. A. J. White, 'The Newlands Pottery Kiln Revisited', *Contrebis*, Vol. XXI, 1996, p. 25; J. W. A. Price, 'The Lancaster Pottery', *Contrebis*, Vol. I, No. 1, 1973. pp. 15–19. In Lancaster a three storey windmill was used in the eighteenth century to grind the colours for the pottery on the Quay. This site (SD 470 620) worked from *c.* 1750–1790, but the buildings survived, marked on Binn's map of 1821 and on the 1st Edition OS of 1844 as Pot House.

53. W. G. Niven, 'Scotforth Pottery', *Contrebis*, Vol. X, 1985, pp. 31–38. Scotforth was thought to have been founded by one Thomas Tatham, *c.* 1840, and was later run by member of the Bateson family (of Burton in Lonsdale). It was eventually acquired by James Williamson.

54. Humphries, 'Industry in Bentham and Thornton', pp. 25–31; A. J. White, *Country Pottery from Burton in Lonsdale* (Lancaster City Museums, Local Studies, no. 10, 1989).

55. H. Bateson, 'Burton Potteries', *Yorkshire History Quarterly*, Vol. 5, No. 2, November 1999.

56. J. Galbraith, 'Portrait of a Country Potter', Unpublised B.Ed. (Hons) Dissertation, St Martins College, Lancaster, 1979.

57. J. W. A. Price, *The Industrial Archaeology of the Lune Valley* (CNWRS, Occasional Paper No. 13, University of Lancaster, 1983), pp. 38–46; Edward Baines, *Directory of Lancashire* (1825) records only one brick house in Lancaster and they were rare in the locality until the late nineteenth century. Mannex directory of 1881 only records five brick works.

58. Adverts in *Lancaster Guardian*, 22 February, 19 & 24 September 1840.

59. Worrall's Directory (1879) lists William Parker, New Butt, Bentham, Tile Manufacturer; Mannex Directory (1881) records this site as Chester's Tile Works.

60. PRO, DDHH BOX No. 14 135/377 Documents of Lunesdale Brick & Tile Co., dated 1897, plans for permissions to construct a bridge over the main road for a ropeway. Plans include builder's estimates (George Pattinson of Windermere), specifications and line of ropeway up to clay pits, plan of brickworks and surrounding farms.

CHAPTER FOUR

Mining 'the Lonsdale Coals'

Phil Hudson

Although the Lune Valley is not usually associated with coal mining, local people were engaged in the sporadic extraction of the 'Lonsdale Coals' over several hundred years. This chapter provides a basic introduction to this activity, focusing on a few sites, so readers interested in delving deeper should consult the author's more detailed illustrated study, published since this chapter was written, *Coal Mining in Lunesdale*.[1]

The coalfield

Geographically 'Lonsdale Coal' seams stretch over a large area, from Ellel and Scotforth in the south, west to the coast at Bazil Point, Overton, then northwards to Lancaster, Halton, Whittington and Hutton Roof. Easterly they stretch up through Littledale, Quernmore, Caton, Tatham, the Hindburn and Roeburn valleys and on into the area around Bentham, Burton, Ingleton and Mewith. Further north and east they extend to the Barbon and Casterton Fells and the eastern slopes of Whernside, Dent and Garsdale.

The largest, deepest mines with the longest working lives were localised in the Burton-Ingleton[2] area, and are associated with the geology of the Great Scar fault, and the coarse Red Sandstones and Conglomerates.[3] This 'Ingleton coalfield' is some four square miles in extent, and lies within the parishes of Burton in Lonsdale, Bentham, Ingleton and Thornton in Lonsdale.[4] But these mines worked a different coal seam than the majority of those down the valley which are the main subject in this chapter and about which comparatively little has been written.[5]

Field evidence of the remains of drift workings, bell-pits, shaft heads, spoil heaps, adits and associated buildings, roads and trackways suggests there have been many attempts to mine the minor seams in the rest of Lonsdale. In many of the locations the coal seams outcrop or occur just below the surface. The remains of these bell-pit types of workings are featured in the landscape today as small circular depressions which vary between 8 and 30 feet across, with a surface rim of spoil often only a few inches high and perhaps three yards or so in width. Some operations, however, reached a respectable size. Many of these landscape features are now well grassed over when seen in open fields, often nearly ploughed out or filled in through years of weathering or the damaging actions of animals' feet. Others have been deliberately filled in by farmers or landowners during land improvement schemes, or used as convenient rubbish dumps. The process has been going on for a long time. In Quernmore, where many of the old mine workings have been destroyed, filled in and levelled over the years, the earliest recorded dates back to 1792 when one of Lancaster Corporation's pits was filled.[6] Several old workings were landscaped as recently as 1980 on land to the side of Gresgarth Hall, with one large spoil heap under the northern scarp (SD 533 633) being preserved by covering it in plastic mesh to stabilise it and then sown with grasses to make a landscape feature within the woodland garden area of the hall grounds. Other sites in Hollinhead Barn Field (SD 534 629) have also been filled, ploughed over and new drains set, but not within living memory. Recently most of the bell-pits and shaft-head spoil has been levelled at Farleton, Russells and School Colliery sites.

Occasionally groupings of pits were given specific names as colliery sites. Both Lancaster Corporation and Hornby Castle Estate often referred to their coal workings as collieries although many were possibly only drifts, single shafts, or the odd bell-pit.[7] 'Colliery' or 'cole pitt' seemed to be the acceptable usage in many of the early source documents in referring to any long or short-term coal mining activity. However, in some cases the geology or topography favoured more intensive workings, with the seams of coal thick enough and near to the surface to be worked more intensively for some time, and on such sites there were deep shafts down to the coal seams and conventional surface gear, although these were still usually accompanied by the other types of working methods, such as bell-pits and levels, further along the coal seams. Examples of named collieries include Mount Vernon (SD 504 845); Ellel (SD 498 532); Rough Lot (SD 526 609); Smear Hall (SD 622 670); Wray Wood (SD 623 657); Clintsfield (SD 629 698); School Colliery (SD 621 688); Farleton (SD 576 675), Botton Coal-pit Lot (SD 655 685) and Greystone Gill (SD 665 685).

The main seam in the district was termed the 'Clintsfield Coal' by Moseley.[8] This has been most extensively worked along a line south of High Bentham and across to Crossdale, but it also extends northwards into the valley of the River Greta. For the most part it is inferior quality, except perhaps at the Blands and Clintsfield, in most of the Tatham colliery sites, and at Greystone Gill, High Bentham (SD 665 685), Moulter Beck (SD 664 685), Coal-pits Close (SD 658 682) and Lanefoot in Tatham Parish. There are also references which suggest that there were some workings up to some 300 feet deep in the Ellel and Scotforth areas.[9] This is not necessarily evidence that there were pits of this depth, however, and probably refers to the depth of the trial borings. However, Ellel has several documented sites. Coal was found at Welby Cragg, Ellel in the early nineteenth century and the *Lancaster Guardian* of 19 November 1837 also reported that coal had been found on the Whams House Estate in Ellel. These reports possibly refer to the rediscovery of old coal seams that were mined in the early eighteenth century and possibly re-worked at that time.

The Whams site's field names support the view that coal was mined here. Field 728 on the 25 inch 1934 O.S. map is called Further Coal Carr; on the 1913 O.S. sheet 39.3 field 1137 is called Coal Carr, and on sheet 39.4 field 1169, situated between the railway line and Whams Lane, is called Coal Pit Field (SD 499 532).

Searching for coal

Quite when coal mining began in the Lune Valley is unclear, but there was almost certainly some activity during the medieval period. However, the earliest reliable record that has been found to date is at Wegber in about 1520.[10] From then until the late eighteenth century coal workings were generally small, local affairs and reliable coal mining records first appear which can link in with identified sites. Nearly all the surviving eighteenth-century publications and diaries which refer to this part of Lancashire make some mention of coal mining or prospecting including Stout,[11] Wilberforce,[12] Cragg[13] and Tyldesley.[14] In the early nineteenth century there were concerted and organised efforts to find the larger, workable coal seams near these earlier workings, and several named colliery sites began long term operations.

Geologically most of the rest of the Lune Valley is blessed with all the correct rock formations and characteristics which should make it a good coal-bearing area. Most of the area's solid geology is 'coal measures'- Millstone Grits and shales, Yordales, with main, middle and underset Limestone and associated coals. These are the kind of geological features under which rich coal seams of economic workable size are found in other areas of northern England. It was these features which led many people in the Lancaster district in the early nineteenth century to believe that most of the Lune Valley had potential for coal mining, and that profitable seams of coal would be found alongside or nearby the already worked minor pits. Much effort was expended in the trial boring for coal, usually in fruitless areas. A well-subscribed and supported public company, based in Lancaster, was formed and maintained an existence until about 1840, culminating in the publishing of Prof. J. Phillips' report on coal in the area. The reasons for this renewed interest are various, and obvious. Most important was the increasing use of coal within the township both domestically and for industry, and its high price. Expensive coal supplies had to be shipped up the Preston-Lancaster canal from the Wigan and south Lancashire coal-fields, or via the sea into the port or outports of Lancaster.[15] Many felt that coal had the potential to reverse the downturn of the local economy after the decline of the port and its associated trade since, further south in the county, cheap coal was increasingly used to generate steam power for gas lighting, and in the textiles and engineering industries.

These efforts did not succeed because contemporaries failed to appreciate the complicated geology of the area which determined why coal-workings remained relatively small and scattered. The area was formed in the Sabdenian Stage which contains the Clintsfield Grit. This is about 45 feet thick and has several coal seams, though none are thought to be more than about two feet in thickness. This is the lowest member of the Bentham Grit group and forms the top of the Sabdenian outcropping between the rivers Roeburn and Hindburn where it is seen as a fairly coarse felspathic sandstone. To the north it becomes flaggy at the lower end and ganisteriod near the top, and the thin lensing coals appear in the middle. In most areas of lower Lunesdale, 'Lonsdale Coal' appears immediately above the gritstones or lodged between differing grit strata, and unless there has been faulting, or other geological upheavals of some kind, such as where some of the dips are over 45 degrees, the coal is either within 60 feet of the surface or, well covered, either with rock strata and overlying glacial material. Overlying deposits can be over 200 feet thick, as is the case with the Upper Caton Shales, and over 600 feet thick in the case of the Roeburndale, Oak Bank Grits, thus making mining of these very difficult.

Unloading coal at Storeys in Lancaster in the early twentieth century. Lancaster's textile mills were all located alongside the canal to enable them to gain easy access to coal. Rural mills were not so fortunate. (*Lancaster City Museums*)

Working the pits

Mining methods vary with the location and strata of the seams worked within the area. Field evidence indicates that several different types of 'shaft' have been sunk. Deeper workings, as at Clintsfield, Smear Hall and Farleton Pits, eventually had the conventional type shaft with all its machinery and gear. A common method of working coal in small pits, however, was to drive down two shafts near to each other. The larger one was used to bring up all the coal, the other smaller one had a fire on top of it which could be tended by the winch-man operating the winch on the larger shaft. The reason for having a fire on the top of the small shaft was that it made it possible to draw air through the mine below and, if a series of barriers or baffles were introduced in the underground works, the miners could move air around where they needed it within the complex. This 'double' bell-pit

Edmondson's Pit, Banksmain, Wray Wood: A double shafted working (see text for details). The width of the shaft, some of the stone lining, the flat area around the rim, and the spoil from the pit are all visible. The Edmondsons of Outhwaite mined coal on their land, which was adjacent to the Hornby Estate's pits. During the 1820s there was some dispute about whose land some of the seams were located under. (Phil Hudson)

arrangement is particularly useful when working coal seams in steeply angled and dipping strata, and is a feature common in the Lonsdale coal workings. It has also been identified at various places in Gibson Wood, Quernmore (SD 526 611), at Banksmain and Burton, on Lythe Brow and Heights areas of Quernmore (SD 529 633). Where coal is near the surface, on hilly ground, yet too deep or awkward to use bell-pits, a different working method was often employed, notably adits and driven levels, where seams were mined horizontally from the side of a hill.

Some sites were 'rearing' type mines. Here the colliers, having discovered an outcrop of coal, worked it by following it down the seam taking out the coal, which was rarely more than two feet thick, without disturbing the rock on either side. Where the dip angle of the seam was very steep, these workings eventually became shafts and could be 50 or 60 feet deep.[16] A good example of this rearing method of working can be seen on the Short Reks site (SD 529 638). Here coal has been found because it out-cropped at a steep angle through the geological faulting and tilting of the grits of the Quernmore syncline. The coal has been worked downwards for up to 80 feet, until the seam was too narrow to work. Close inspection of the shafts on this site show the faulted geological strata, the associated coal measure fossils and the remaining narrowed, unworkable coal seam in the base of the shaft and traces of coal in the niches on the shaft sides. This type of working was possibly employed on other sites, but the landscape evidence for them is often lacking, as there was almost no spoil in connection with them and the final shafts were often refilled and levelled.

Owners, occupiers and workers

Coal mining involved local people right across the social spectrum. Owners of mineral rights ranged from the Lord of Hornby and his successors to the Hornby Castle Estates, the Cliffords at Quernmore Park, the Daltons of Thurnham Hall, immigrant nouveaux-rich like Edmondson at Gresgarth

Hall, Caton, and local businessmen like Thomas Albright in Lancaster.[17] Some local well-established yeoman farming families also became involved in mining including the Gibsons of Hollinhead and the Edmondsons of Outhwaite, who were not related to the Edmondsons of Gresgarth (or Grassyard) Hall.

Some of these local gentry actively prospected for coal in the eighteenth century hoping to open up collieries on their land. The Daltons of Thurnham near Lancaster, for example, invested in coal mining on their lands at Bulk just to the east of Lancaster. Thomas Tyldesley's diary for the year 1713 records several of their attempts.[18] On 15 October 'met bro. Dalton a hunting on Scotforth More, … thence wee went to Hill colliors, who were boring in ye Ling cloas. Gave ym 1 shilling. Bro Dalton wentt home and dined with mee …' On 3 December, 'I went with bro … Dalton to ye Linge Cloase to see Hill(sic) coliors boar. Thence to Wheaton to dinr …', and on 18 December 'went a hunting to Booke (Bulk), Called to see Bror Dalton's borrers; gave ym 6d …' [19] Evidence of their activity is still visible today in some relict remains and field names. In more recent examples, public companies were often formed at the instigation of local worthies to carry out exploration and working of the local coal, as at Lancaster in 1836.[20]

Then there were individuals and co-operatives, often with farming interests, who operated mines on Hutton Roof, or leased mines by agreement with these local landowners or from Lancaster Corporation on Quernmore Common and Lancaster Moor. In some areas it is possible that a local tradition of coal mining was established, as was the case among some families in the Casterton-Barbon area who acquired expertise which was used elsewhere. One Edward Taylor, for example, collier of Casterton, opened a mine on Lancaster Moor on a lease from Lancaster Corporation in 1763.

It is more difficult to find out much about the men and boys who actually worked the mines. The Hornby Castle muniments and George Smith's diary [21] contain the names of the many people in connection with mining on the estate up to 1831, but do not always give an address, although it is possible to deduce from one set of papers, connected with a mining dispute in 1824 on Wray Wood Moor, that quite a number of men and boys were engaged in the pits there.[22] The census figures of 1831 list 41 men working as coal miners in the parishes of Wray, Roeburndale and Tatham.[23] This is perhaps the highest figure employed, at least as far as those potentially considered to be full-time colliers and labourers, but there must also have been many part time dual-occupation workers as well. The figures for 1841 show a decline with only 27 coal miners, and by 1851 only 13 are recorded in Wray and two in Tatham, plus a Mr John Kelly, born in Dublin, listed as a mining surveyor who was staying with William Cornthwaite of Wray.

The census of 1841 lists people engaged in mining at the following addresses. In Wray Township, 21 named miners: at Lane Dyke, John, Joseph and Richard Berry; at Scuttle Hill, William and Richard Howson; at Stauvin, William and John Howson the two sons of Anthony who is listed as a farmer. In Tatham at Sod Hall, there was Thomas Balderston; at MillHouse, James Wildman and Robert Hodgson; at Houtly, Robert Lowder; at Perry Moor, William Wildman; at Bridge End, William Hall; at Moor End, James Taylor and at Moorside, Robert Balderstone, making a total of 36 recorded in the two townships. What is noticeable is that although some of the addresses are familiar, most of the names recorded in the Hornby Muniments in the first two decades of this century are absent. There are no Edmondsons, Batesons, Armitsteads, Bowskills, Browns, Sauls, Burrows, Charnleys, Gills, Corts, Fayrers, Knowles, Eccles, Carrs or Procters.

The Bentham census for 1841 also records some 40 men and boys with occupations connected to coal mining and in the absence of any other documentary evidence, it is perhaps safe to assume a similar level of coal mining in this township at this date. The figure for 1851 is just twelve. Just where these people were working is not known, but scattered around the parish there are the remains of a number of bell-pits and spoil heaps, the field evidence of several coalpits. Family names associated with coal mining extracted from the Bentham parish registers between 1760–1800 yield another ten individuals – Harker, Hodgson, Wildman, Carr, Brown, Thornton, Harrison, Johnson, Bullock and Leeming – suggesting some long-term working perhaps with family connections. The last mentioned, the Leemings, started with David in 1792 and ended with Thomas in 1851. But, like the other examples quoted above, the old family names do not endure past mid-century. Of those in 1851 only the one Leeming survives, one other William Bullock, aged 54, had moved to Ingleton as a working coal miner.

Fireman (H. Capstick), Waterside Pottery: An atmospheric interior photograph from the mid-twentieth century of a worker who is often overlooked in histories of coal and steam – the fireman. (*Lancaster City Museums*/Henry Bateson)

Some major sites

Caton collieries

The so-called 'Caton Collieries', on what Moseley called the 'Caton Coal Seams', were first worked in the sixteenth century and again in the eighteenth and nineteenth centuries.[24] This coal seam straddles the Caton-Quernmore-Littledale boundary with the coal being found on either side of the Artle Beck fault. Here, where there is a lack of continuity in the rock strata, coal has been exposed, or runs very near to the surface. The main locations where this coal has been worked are Gresgarth (often referred to in older documents as Grassyard), Short Reks, Hollinhead, Haws House in Caton-Littledale parish and in north Quernmore at the Hagg, William Bank, Scroggs, Askew Hill, Gibson Wood and Rough Lot. These workings are mentioned in Baines' directory of 1825[25] and that of Mannex in 1881.[26]

Gresgarth Hall was part of the ancient Curwen family's lands who held half the moiety of Caton with Littledale and occupied the estate from 1330 to the early seventeenth century. The estate then changed hands several times after the last in the male Curwen line died about 1633.[27] There is no known surviving documentary evidence for coal mining on the estate during this time, despite the fact that the family was related to the Curwens of north Cumbria who were owners of the collieries and mines. As far as can be ascertained, from the archives consulted, there were no specific references to any coal mining within the Quernmore Park lands until the estate was owned by the Clifford family in the late seventeenth century.

There is, however, some evidence of coal mining, both legal and illegal, outside the medieval parks, but within the Royal Forest Lands, by the freemen, burgesses and Corporation of Lancaster, on Lancaster Moor and Quernmore Common. The Minute Books of Lancaster Corporation show income from the town's drift mine on the moor and coal mines in Quernmore from before 1680. Between 1661 and 1736 entries in the Corporation Minutes for royalties received from the drift of Quernmore range from nothing to 19s. 4d. per annum, but no output figures are recorded.[28] In 1689, 1690 and 1691 Isaac Blackburn paid the Corporation of Lancaster a rent of £2 10s. 0d. per annum for a colliery. He gave it up in 1710 when it was offered to a Mr Mayor (a William Meyer appears in a Claughton mining agreement of 1693) and his partners at £50 per annum for two years, extending to 5, 7 or 21 years as convenient, but with the provisio that he was not to assign to any other person during the term without consent.[29]

The earliest record of any mining activity in Gresgarth is in documents listed in Lancashire Papists Estates.[30] These show that the workings were leased or let to a local syndicate of miners and farmers in 1714, when Edward Riddell of Swinburne Castle, Northumberland, Lord of the Manor of Caton, let a colliery at Grassyard to Thomas Jackson, Thomas

Gibson Wood and Rough Lot coalpits, Rigg Lane, Quernmore: The remains of the stone quarries in this area can clearly be seen by walkers from the path leading up Clougha from the car park on Rigg Lane but the existence of coal mines below the road is more difficult to appreciate. (Phil Hudson)

Cornthwaite and William and John Nicholson for 21 years from 11 November 1714. Rent was £24 yearly, and under reservation of 10 guineas to Dorothy wife of Edward Riddell, out of the first coals that should be wrought to that value.[31] In the Gaisford collection[32] there is another lease dated 13 January 1731, which is for six years at a rent of £18, again from Thomas Riddell, for the collieries on his estate of Grassyard let to men in Caton and Quernmore.[33] These workings appear to have been more than just opencast or small bell type pits, as the lease document contains some instructions for the support of the roof, controlling water and making access roads. In another Gaisford document, dated 2 May 1741, the Grassyard and Hawkshead colliery was let by Thomas Riddell to Richard Gibson, yeoman farmer of Hollinhead, for seven years at a rent of £12 12s.[34] These could be the pits seen in Hollinhead Barn Field (SD 534 629).

In the early eighteenth century, the Rawlinsons acquired land in the Caton-Quernmore area and started the Caton Forge in 1727. Abraham Rawlinson is mentioned as buying the north part of Hollinhead Estate from Richard Gibson in 1750.[35] These, and other Rawlinson documents, mention coal mining and suggest that the estate may have had pits to the south of Oak Cottage. Further evidence is found in the Caton fragment of deeds for Hollinhead lands that indicate Rawlinson held Gresgarth and several other estates in the area by 1763.[36] As far as continuity of working the Caton seams is concerned, there is no further documentary evidence until the Grassyard estate was put up for sale in 1801, when the following advert appeared in the *Lancaster Gazette* for 26 September 1801: 'For sale Grassyard Park, Hall, land and collieries included'.

Farleton, Tatham and Smear Hall

Hornby Castle Estate owned many sites in lower Lonsdale but only four – Farleton, Tatham Smearhaw (or hall) and Clintsfield[37] – are known for certain to have had steam-powered, mechanically-driven lifting or pumping gear, stone built-associated pit head buildings, cinder ovens and access roads.

Farleton Colliery site (SD 576 675) is the first one mentioned in the written record as early as 1565.[38] 'To Edward Cookson (or Collison?) for the rental of the Coyle mines in Farleton at xx. s by the year, behind unpaid for iiij years and a halfe … Due in Anno Vij Elizabeth, 1565, as appeareth in the roll of the same year'.[39] The last phase of working started when the pit was re-opened by William Procter and John Eccles in late 1829, and new buildings and equipment installed. George Smith's diary for 12 April 1831 records, 'I measured the masonry for the Engine House at Farleton Colliery done by John Houlding', and on 27 August, 'Engine commenced at Farleton Colliery'. Nothing remains today since after abandonment the winding house and other surface buildings were demolished and pushed into the shaft to seal it.

There were extensive workings in Lower Tatham extending over many acres which were operated at different times between 1642 and 1841.[40] Some were worked by the Hornby Castle Estate since George Smith regularly recorded his trips to 'Tatham Colliery' to supervise the workings, collect dues or make payments, but others appear to have been operated by lessees or owned by local farmers. Among the named pit sites are several which must have been close to residences which still survive, such as Meggs, School Hill, School House, Russells and Parkside. Various methods of extraction would appear to have been employed. We know, for example, that there was an adit working across the road from the Bridge Inn, since its remains are just visible. (SD 612 694). Smith also makes references to equipment, although it is difficult to know precisely where on the site these were located. Entries for 'Tatham Pit' in late 1823 or and early 1824 show that there was a pit house and that a horse was used for 'pulling coals'. During the same period there are also references to 'the engine house at Tatham' and a steam boiler which was probably used for pumping off the water which plagued the workings. There were also ovens on the site which produced cinders to sell to the local population.[41]

The last pit to work the Lonsdale Coals outside the Ingleton coalfield was Smear Hall, sometimes referred to as Smearhaw, at one time the principal colliery of Hornby Castle Estates. This was working from about 1780 until it closed in 1882 when an abandonment plan was lodged.[42] The last operator was T. B. Kayes who had two pits of 13 and 16 yards depth. Most of the coal by this stage would appear to have been got from near

Main Coal Mining Sites in Tatham (opposite) (Phil Hudson)

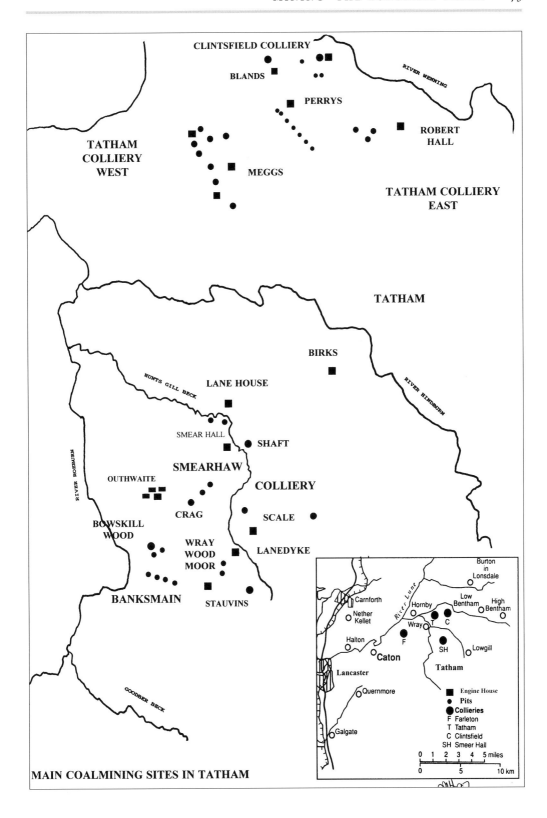

MAIN COALMINING SITES IN TATHAM

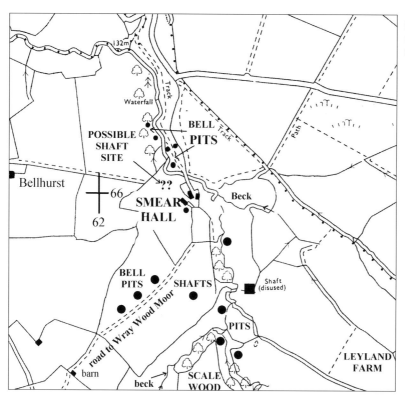

Smear Hall Colliery
(Phil Hudson, adapted
from OS 25 inch map)

the surface, but Hornby Estate's Collieries Account book for 1834–38 has
several entries for it and Smith's diaries reveal that it had deep shafts,
although it is difficult to locate these precisely today, and that its underground workings were regularly extended. There are no extant buildings
although, like several others, the site is known to have had a set of cinder
ovens where coal was roasted to produce something like modern day coke.
Smith records that these ovens required regular attention. He also records
several labour disputes in the 1820s when men demanded better pay.

Clintsfield

Further up the valley of the Wenning, at Clintsfield colliery (SD 629 698),
there are the remains of extensive colliery buildings including an engine
house, an adjoining earlier building, traces of a pond, water races, waterwheel pits, a horse gin base, raised metalled roadways, a bridge over the
river to the north, and to south and west bell-pits, or older shaft heads
(although some could have been iron mines) with spoil heaps. Although
this site was situated on land owned in the nineteenth century by the
Gerrard family it was linked in a variety of ways with the Hornby Estate
workings, since it is mentioned several times in George Smith's diaries.
The mine appears to be one of the more lasting and extensive of the lower
Lune Valley workings as well as the best preserved.

The site is first recorded in a lease of 1772 and is shown on Yates' map in 1786 as a working coal mine with a building and water wheel (i.e. a pithead wheel). The mine was still open in 1822 and the pit was raising coal and producing cinders for sale in 1835.[43] The site was still working in 1836.[44] The surviving stone buildings, however, are later structures. The stone engine house was built in 1839 for the lessees, by one Arthur Burrows, who lived at Blands Farm.[45] Since the mine closed this building has been altered and used as a dwelling before being abandoned and left to decay. The complete structure once housed winding/pumping gear, with a steam boiler to provide power for a steam driven engine.[46] It is set in a hollow and joined to the earlier buildings, surrounded by what appears to be the old pit spoil. The east gable is built mainly of cut stone blocks; the rest is random freestone with cut quoins. The adjoining boiler house has a chimney. The square-built chimney, which could be contemporary with the boiler house to which it is attached at the south west corner, is now topped and capped with a stone slate roof and measures 10 feet. square. It still stands some 18 feet. high. This, and the rest of the building range, are thought to be earlier than the Burrows addition; all are now without a roof. The east wall of the winding/engine house is mainly built of large cut stone blocks, with corner quoins, and measures 18 feet by 19 feet with some 20 feet of gables intact. It has an upper-arched opening for the gear, which has been partly walled to take a later square window, and a lower doorway in the east end, a window and a doorway with traces of a porch on the south, upper and lower windows in the west gable, which were possibly cut when the building was converted to a house before 1861, evidence of which also remains as surviving internal plastering, fireplaces and floor joists.[47] There is an original doorway in the lower part of the north wall to give access to the attached boiler house. The roof was stone slated, but all except the eaves-wallheads have gone. One internal wooden roof truss and some cast iron pieces were still on site when it was first visited in 1967. The attached lean-to boiler house to the north measures 40 feet by 13 feet; the

Clintsfield Colliery, Engine House, 1995: This site is the only one with substantial remains of the district's scattered coal mining industry. (Phil Hudson)

size can still be seen in the extant foundations. It has cut corner quoins and rubble walling, but there are no gables extant or windows and the east wall has gone with the tops crumbling. The base of the north wall has burnt stonework and is slightly concave inside where the boiler was housed. There is evidence of the pit shaft in the depression on the east side and there are remains of a banked pond to the north.

The Burrows were also involved in coal mining at Blands Farm pits. An undated newspaper cutting refers to the personal coal mine of Arthur Burrows at Blands Farm (SD 625 697).[48] This is a shaft situated in the large hollow behind the house covered by a large stone slab. Site inspection suggests that the coal here has been extensively worked, and there are the mysterious walled tunnels and shafts nearby which appear to have been connected with coal working.[49]

Greystone Gill

One coal mine for which we have a particular good account is at Greystone Gill (SD 682 689) in High Bentham and this can be used to show the relatively precarious and small-scale nature of operations, as well as the range of people involved. This is a site on an estate purchased by George Wright in 1816 from the Titterington Trustees.[50] He then used the expertise of George Smith, whom he had under his control as Steward of Hornby Castle, to develop a colliery on the site. George Smith's diary records the progress.

In late 1819 a Henry Towers calls on him 'respecting the coal at Greystone Gill' and is then employed as overseer by Wright to begin the works. In January 1820 Charles Jaques and two others are employed to drive a level, work which they finished on 20 May when Wright made a final settlement. Henry Towers and an Alexandra Caton continued to be employed on the site as it developed and in June 1820 a new road was made; this work is carried out by John Towers and a Mr Bowker. Thomas Bowskill, the Hornby Estate's 'Master Collier' was also involved in the more technical works along with George Smith and on 25 July 1820 they began to try new levels, one of them situated at 'The Holme'. There was a lot of activity at this time, Bowskill and Smith were ever present, the estate carpenters were cutting wood for props and making 'boring pumps', and E. Knowles was set to work preparing the pumps etc., to go in the shaft. By 15 September there was another level open from the 'Winning', extending to some 8 yards, and on the 10 October the first two cart-loads of coals were got and promptly taken to George Wright's house at Heysham by Thomas Bleazard, the Hornby Castle Estates carter. On 22 November 1820 for some reason, Wright ordered activities to cease, and Smith wrote in his diary: 'Henry Towers called about Grastine,(sic. Greystone) Gill colly. Mr Wright ordered that the pumping and driving should cease this weekend'. However, the new year saw renewed activity. On 10 January 1821, Wright hired George Becket, Robert Workman and Alexandra Caton to sink a new coal shaft,

Greystone Gill Colliery
(Phil Hudson, adapted
from OS 25 inch map)

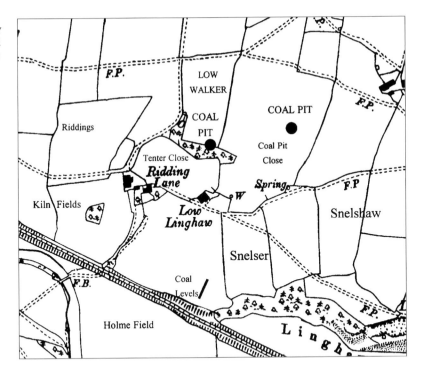

and Wright also promised to pay them five and halfpence per load for getting the coals. Work proceeded and on 1 February 1822, '22 cart loads of coal were fetched from Graystone Gill to Hornby'. Thereafter there are frequent references to activity including the sinking of a shaft (17 & 24 February 1822); deficient accounts and the sacking of Towers, the colliery banksman, who would seem to have been selling coal from the site (31 December 1822); and the sinking of another pit (8 March 1823).

Then in January 1824 everything stopped, presumably on Wright's order, and the site was cleared and the pits filled in. Smith recorded in his diary, 'Jan 8th Thursday 1824 James Armitstead and Alex Caton having finished filling up the coal pits at Greystone Gill called and I paid them ...' But the site later appears to have been taken over by a partnership. Smith records: 'July 15th 1828 John Tittinton (Titterington?) and Thomas Thompson called taking Graystone Gill Colly' and on 'Feb 9th 1829 John Cumberland came and borrowed the pump boring tools for Graystone Gill Colliery Company.' And again, on 'Jan 2nd 1830 Robert Titterington, Richard Marshall and John Cumberland called at the Castle and paid up the rent of Graystone Gill Colliery. Marshall and Cumberland took the colliery again for 4 years at £25 per year, but to give it up by a month's notice, term to commence on 4th inst.' 'Feb 5th 1831 Richard Marshall of Bentham called and paid me a years rent for Greystone Gill Colliery' suggesting that the colliery was worked by them for at least another three years. Unfortunately there are no more references to the site, but a map by John Binns dated 1831 of Wright's Estate marks the two coal pits in the field north of Lower Lingow.

The Upper Lune Valley

Coal seams have long been worked in the townships of Dent, Garsdale, Casterton and Barbon, working a thin seam of poor quality coal. Members of the Sedbergh Historical Society have researched and published on Dentdale and Garsdale.[51] The pits in Cowgill appear to have been re-opened in the late nineteenth century on lease to various individuals and partnerships and were then worked off and on for over 70 years. The pits in Garsdale were earlier, dating from *c.* 1650, and were mainly located on Baugh Fell, where over 110 disused pits, and associated buildings, crofts and roads, that follow a line parallel with the Dent Fault, have been mapped and recorded by Lancaster. These pits were all closed, as uneconomical, once the railway was brought through the area in 1861.

The Casterton and Barbon workings were documented as working from the mid-eighteenth century until about 1860. Field remains have been examined by the present author, but little documentary source material has been found. The earliest reference to a date for Casterton is 1766, and for Barbon, 1761, but Bulmer states that the Casterton mines had been working from the mid-seventeenth century.[52] Talbot-Aveline (et al) mentions the coals of the area in the Geological Survey 1872.[53] A document in Kendal Record Office, states that the Earls of Lonsdale were lessees of the Richmond fee which gave them legal claim to coal workings on Casterton Fell. These pits (SD 675 820), are shown on the maps as old shafts running on a line north to south. Seven are recorded between Ease Gill and Hazel Syke, and closer inspection could well give some useful insights into working methods. Smith's diary for 25 September 1823 records that 'Joseph Gill called to ask leave to go to bore a pit at Barbon for one Robinson, but I refused to let him go'.[54] Gill later in the year gave up his employment at Hornby and his house at Goodber, so it is presumed that he went to work at Robinson's Barbon Pit. On 7 November 1823 Smith wrote, 'William Atkinson and John Porter took Thomas Hall at Barbon Coal Pits'. Hall was a fugitive from the justices, but he appears to be a Barbon man so he easily found work in the isolated moorland pits, hoping to avoid the two constables searching for him.[55] The Barbon pits were still working in 1831 when a fatality was recorded in the *Lancaster Gazette*.[56]

There are several workings in the general area to the north of Gragareth and Whernside centred on SD 690 830. Mining-related place-names abound: Coal Pits Hill, Colliers Lane, Colliers Syke, Old Pit, Old Pit Track, Three Gills Pit. Two seams have been worked on Gragareth, one between the Main and Underset Limestone near Binks Great Coombe and Crag Side, which runs into the south-west corner of the crag. The coal worked at Three Gills Pit was probably the lower. Both seams occur between Short Gill and Hazel Sike, but the geology makes the workings irregular and limited in extent. Around the horizon, Prof. Phillips described coal at Cotter Fell which '... varies in thickness from 8 to 13 inches ... coal affected and not found all round the hill ... The second seam which has been extensively worked is the lowest coal in the Yoredales ... occurs in the Middle Limestone. In one pit the seam was 4 to 5 inches thick, in another 6 inches, but in adjoining pits from 15 to 20 inches and of good quality.' A map dated 1835 shows a coal pit on Ease Gill.[57] These old pits and workings were surveyed by Kay-Shuttleworth's mining engineer in the 1850s but, like many of the physical remains of pits throughout Lonsdale, the reports have been lost.

Notes

1. P. J. Hudson, *Coal Mining in Lunesdale* (Hudson History, Procter House, Kirkgate, Settle, 1998).

2. J. Bentley, 'An Introduction to Ingleton Coalfield and Colliery', *Contrebis*, Vol. XX, 1995, pp. 35–38.

3. Professor John Phillips, *Report on the Probability of the Occurrence of Coal and other Minerals in the Vicinity of Lancaster* (W. Barwick, Lancaster. 1837). Professor Phillips suggest these seams also equate with the ones found on Fountains Fell and Pen-y-gent.

4. A. Harris, 'The Ingleton Coalfield', *Industrial Archaeology*, Vol. 5 (no. 4), 1969, pp. 313–347; M. Humphries, 'The Development and Decline of Industry in the Ancient Parishes of Bentham and Thornton in Lonsdale in the Nineteenth Century', Unpublished Local History Diploma Dissertation, Liverpool University (in Lancaster Univ. Library), 1984; M. Humphries, 'Some Notes on Coal mining in Burton in Lonsdale', *Contrebis*, Vol. XX, 1995, pp. 25–34; T. D. Ford, 'The Upper Carboniferous Rocks of the Ingleton Coalfield', *Quarterly Journal of the Geological Society*, 1954.

5. J. Clare, & P. J. Hudson, 'Notes on Coal and Coal Mining in Western Lunesdale and Quernmore', *Contrebis*, Vol. XIII, 1986/7, pp. 2–17; P. J. Hudson, 'Landscape and Economic Development of Quernmore Forest, Lancaster: An Upland Marginal Area in North West Lancashire to *c.* 1850'. Unpublished M.Phil thesis, University of Lancaster, 1994, chapter 9, pp. 284–321. Passing references are made in M. E. Butler, 'A Survey of the Geographical Factors that have controlled the History of Lonsdale', Unpublished M.A. thesis, 1921, p. 56; J. W. A. Price, *The Industrial Archaeology of the Lune Valley* (CNWRS, University of Lancaster, Occasional Paper No. 13, 1983).

6. Lancaster Corporation Minute Book, 4 December 1792.'It is ordered that the mayor and bailiffs contract with some person to fill up the coal pits or shafts in Quernmore belonging to the corporation which are now open and dangerous'.

7. P. J. Hudson, 'Some Notes on the Hornby Castle Estate Coal Mining Sites', *British Mining*, Vol. 50, Memoirs 1994, pp. 111–43; Lancaster Corporation Minute Book, 1661–1736.

8. F. Moseley, 'The Namurian of the Lancaster Fells', *Quarterly Journal of the Geological Society*, Vol. 14 (no. 4), 1953.

9. *Lancaster Gazette*, 9 September 1824.

10. W. Farrer & J. Brownbill (eds), *The Victoria County History of Lancashire* (1906–11), Vol. 1, p. 288b.

11. J. D. Marshall (ed.), *The Autobiography of William Stout of Lancaster, 1665–1752* (Chetham Society Transactions, Vol. 14, Manchester University Press, 1967), p. 258.

12. E. Wrangham (ed.), 'W. Wilberforce's Journey to the Lake District from Cambridge; A Summer Diary 1779', *Oriel*, 1983.

13. LRO, DDX/760/1, Timothy Cragg: Family Memo Book 1698–1816.

14. J. Gillow & A. Hewitson (eds), *The Tyldesley Diary, 1712–1714* (Preston, 1873).

15. Diary of George Smith (hereafter GSD), Hornby Castle Muniments, p. 532: 5 June 1840, 'Coal vessel from Lytham came up the Heysham Lake this evening'; 6 June, 'Mr Wright was busy with horses, carts and men getting the coals from the vessel that came last night.' T. Albright, letter in *Lancaster Gazette*, 20 January 1825.

16. Rearing type workings are found in the Burnley coalfield, the Mountaine Mine (SD 747 334) is a good example, so this mining method is known in north-west Lancashire.

17. E. Baines, *Directory of Lancashire*, 1825, Vol. 2, p. 39; P. J. Hudson, 'A Previously Unrecorded Silk Mill in the Lower Lune Valley', *Contrebis*, Vol. XVIII, 1993, pp. 46–51. Thomas Albright had several business interests beside coal prospecting, also trading as a silk spinner, insurance broker and mill owner.

18. Gillow & Hewitson, *Tyldesley Diary*, p. 118.

19. There is a Ling Cloase marked as a field in Taylors Farm, Bulk, a holding outside the common lands, and a Ling Cloase Gate adjoining which gives access to the Quernmore Common on a pre-enclosure award map of *c.* 1800.

20. *Lancaster Gazette*, 21 July 1836.

21. GSD, Saturday 31 August 1822, 'Thomas Charnley, Joseph Gill and John Hodgson bored thro the coal in Troughton Pasture, thickness of the coal estimated at 19 inches, depth to it 50 yards.'

22. P. J. Hudson, 'The 19th-Century Wray Wood Moor Colliery and Mining Dispute', *British Mining*, Vol. 55, 1995, pp. 81–89.

23. D. M. Clark, 'The Economic and Social Geography of Rural Lonsdale 1801–61', Unpublished MA Thesis, University of Liverpool, 1968.

24. F. Moseley, 'Erosion Surfaces in the Forest of Bowland, Yorks', *Proceedings of the Geological Society*, Vol. 33, 1961, pp. 173–96; W. H. Chippindall, 'A Sixteenth Century Survey & Year's Accounts of the Estates of Hornby Castle', *Chetham Society*, NS., Vol. 102, 1939. The survey records 'to the Lord of the Manor of Hornby to have in Caton a quarry of cole and another of slate … rent of a mine of coal in Farleton.'

25. E. Baines, *History, Directory and Gazetteer of Lancashire* (1825).

26. P. Mannex & Co., *Topography of Lancaster and 16 Miles Around* (Preston, 1881).

27. W. T. W. Potts, 'The Origin of Gresgarth Hall Estate and the Date of Gresgarth Hall', *Contrebis*, Vol. XI, 1983, pp. 26–31.

28. Lancaster Corporation Minute Book. *c.* 1661–1736, p. 70. List of income from the pits in Quernmore.

29. Lancaster Corporation Minute Book, 19 May 1710. Whether the options were taken up is not stated.

30. Lancashire Papists Estates, 5th Roll, 1717.

31. The family names of Jackson and Cornthwaite are found on the tenants' lists of the Quernmore Park Estate at this time and these families also have named holdings adjoining these mining sites on the *c.* 1760 map of Quernmore Park.

32. LRO, DDGa, 23, No. 4.

33. In the Richmond wills collection there is the will proved in 1768 of William Clementson, Caton, collier.

34. LRO, DDGa, 23, No. 5; DDGa, No. 9. This file contains another eighteenth century but undated document attached to the Hollinhead Estate Deeds for Owlers or Ellers Tenements which makes reference to coal mining rights, but is not more specific.

35. This family of Gibsons are no relation to the Gibsons who purchase the Quernmore Park Estates in the late eighteenth. century.

36. LRO, Gaisford Papers, maps, DDGa21/3 and DDGa/13.

37. GSD, 12 April 1831, 'I measured the masonry for the Engine House at Farleton Colliery done by John Houlding.' 17 May 1826, 'I went to the engine house at Tatham where we broke up 42 cwt of old cast iron for some potters.' 28 July 1834, 'I went to Smearhaw and with J. Hodgson looked over and sketched the ground in regard to a new breadth to be got with a steam engine.'

38. P. J. Hudson, 'The Hornby Castle Estate Coal Mines', *Regional Bulletin* (CNWRS), New Series, No. 10, Summer 1996, pp. 72–83.

39. Hornby Castle Muniments, A Rental Document, Elizabeth I, dated 1565.

40. Hornby Castle Muniments, Account Book, 1642, p. 15; GSD, 4 May 1841.

41. GSD, 17, 24, 29 May 1824; 24 December 1827; 20 September 1833; 3 February 1838.

42. NMRS, J/M 233, Scale to 1/10,560.

43. GSD, 29 March 1822, 'Arthur Cort paid me £20.3.0. for rent due to the Rev. Procter (for Clintsfield)'. This rent is almost the same figure as the lease agreement dated 1778, before Cort took over, and is a clue to the owner of the coal mining rights. They could be vested in the Tatham Chapel advowson, 27 August 1835, 'Arthur Cort called and I paid him for Cinders for Wennington Mill.'

44. GSD, 19 April 1836, 'In the morning I went to Millhouses where James Newbys goods were to be sold to day thence to near Clintsfield where I met Richard Fayrer (sic), the overseer, who promised pay the rent.'

45. GSD, 12 October 1839, 'I went to Clintsfield and measured the New Engine House for stone and walling on the part of Arthur Burrows and for carting on the part of Robert Frayer and Thomas Alderson.'

46. Action of the estate of Mr Arthur Cort, a bankrupt, on Monday 30 December 1839 includes: Lot 7: moiety of an engine of 5 h. p., with the boiler, pump and apparatus at Clintch Field (Clintsfield), in the occupation of Richard Farer. There is some slight problem with this date as Arthur Cort's affairs were not wound up until 1846, when there is a reference to this in Smith's Diary (p. 713).

47. The 1861 Census of Population lists under Tatham: "Engine House, Clintsfield, John Travis aged 33 Agricultural Labourer; wife Ann aged 29; and three children William aged 13, Robert aged 12, and Jane 5 months."

48. Lancaster Reference Library, Scrap Book 2, Fol. 49.

49. P. J. Hudson & D. Holmes, 'Blands Revisited', *Contrebis*, Vol. XXI, 1996, pp. 26–8.

50. For details of George Wright's affairs see E. Garnett, *John Marsden's Will: The Hornby Castle Dispute, 1780–1840* (Hambledon Press, London, 1988).

51. D. Bolton, 'The Colliers of Dentdale', *Sedbergh Local Historian*, Vol. 2 (no. 5), 1990, pp. 36–41; K. J. Lancaster, 'Mines and Quarries on Baugh Fell', *Sedbergh Local Historian*, Vol. 2 (no. 4), 1989, pp. 15–20.

52. Kirkby Lonsdale Parish Burial Register, 24 April 1761: John Frankland a stranger, killed by fall into a coal pit near Barbon; Marriage Register, 26 May 1766: John

Nicholls, collier and Mary Taylor both Casterton; Bulmer, *Directory of Lancaster*, p. 446.

53. W. Talbot Aveline, T. M. Hughes & R. H. Tiddeman, *Memoirs of the Geological Survey of England and Wales, Explanation of Quarter Sheet 98 S.E. Kirkby Lonsdale and Kendal* (Longmans Green, 1872).

54. Joseph Gill often appeared in the Hornby records in connection with coal mining, see above the reference to him, with others, working at Troughton Pasture Pit in August 1822.

55. Thornton Parish Burial Registers, 26 July 1806: Lucy wife of Thomas Hall of Barbon in Parish of Kirkby Lonsdale, collier aged 25 years.

56. *Lancaster Gazette*, 3 December 1831 reports one Adam Braithwaite killed at Barbon Colliery through a fall of the roof.

57. PRO, DDHH box 16, map of Casterton Fell by H. Teal, 1834, shows a coal pit to north of Peat Road on Ease Gill.

CHAPTER FIVE

Basket-Making

Emmeline Garnett

Basket-making is a universal craft. There can be no human culture (if we consider the weaver birds there are even animal cultures) which has not discovered how to interlace materials into structures suitable for holding, carrying, catching, storing, fencing and furnishing. In the beginning the materials used were naturally those found near at hand; therefore Lune Valley people were necessarily osier basket-makers, using the shoots of *Salix viminalis* (in some of its many varieties) which grew wild in the ever-changing wetlands of the Lune river bed.

As methods of trade and transport grew more sophisticated, allowing specialisation and the seeking of wider markets, they also allowed for the import of raw material, and these factors turned what had been for many centuries a local craft into a small industry, fixed to a surprising extent in one village, Arkholme, and to one family, the Irelands, but with another colony connected to the pottery industry of Burton. The same factors allowed a completely different industry, the making of oak swills, to be imported from the Lake District into Wray village, where it flourished between 1890 and the 1950s. These two crafts both come under the umbrella of the title of this article, but they had no overlap in production, destination, materials, or workers, and will be dealt with separately.

'An inferior hidden sort of handicraft business'

The original, indigenous craft of making osier baskets dates from that time 'to which the memory of man runneth not to the contrary', in the old legal phrase. A list of mediaeval surnames deriving from occupation suggests Skepper, Busseler, Lepmaker, Panniermaker, Corbiler; but offers over 150 different names derived from the woollen trade.[1]

Against the background of a country area such as the Lune Valley, it cannot have been a specialism, any more than building stone fences or thatching roofs or making bread or clipping sheep. People must have collected the wild materials as they needed them and under much the same rules as pertained to the gathering of firewood. An entry in a Hornby Castle court book for 1585, when the 'New Parke' had just been established, finds the keeper of the park presenting various tenants for gathering wood there. (As no fines were imposed, it is probable that this was a warning to indicate that the 'new parke' was under different rules from the old

common.) One man had felled an oak sapling, two had gathered firewood;
Steven Thomasses was presented for 'one burthen of spelks' and Brian
Williamson for 'one burthen of wands', both words indicating material for
baskets. It was something people did as part of the ordinary pattern of
living, and they did it well or badly according to their degree of ham-
fistedness. Even a national survey of 1747 calls it 'an inferior Hidden Sort
of Handicraft Business'.[2]

This is underlined by the fact that it has proved impossible to retrieve
any evidence for basket-making as an identifiable occupation in the area
until the eighteenth century. In Lancashire, the Parish Register Society has
published 139 volumes (to 1996). Appending trade or status to the names
in parish records was a patchy business, depending on the whim of the
clerk or incumbent, but all the volumes include an index of such trades
as are mentioned. The term 'basket maker' (or in one case 'wisket maker'
and in another 'wand weaver') occurs just 23 times, the first in 1756, most
in the nineteenth century.[3]

The extant Lancaster marriage bonds from 1648 to 1755 have been
published by the Record Society. There are about 15,000 of them. It was
common to give the bridegroom's occupation, often the bondsman's as
well. Four people are identified as 'basket-maker', two of them from one
Caton family, and another from Lancaster, all in the 1730s and 40s.[4] In
1757 all males between 18 and 50 became eligible for militia service, and
the list for South Lonsdale, divided by townships, is extant. For some
reason the 572 names in Lancaster town have their occupations attached.
There are no basket-makers.[5] In the course of abstracting many hundreds
of South Lonsdale wills and inventories for other purposes, mostly before
1800, I have not come across a person called a basket-maker or one who
might be assumed to be one.[6]

In London, with its tightly controlled and organised trades, basket-
making was more recognised as a specialism, though not a very important
one. A list of crafts dating from 1422 puts it in seventy-sixth place.[7] A
Basket-Makers' Company was not established until 1569, and it was a very
small, poor Company. 'Strangers and aliens borne out of this Realme have
not onelie within this honourable Cittie, but also in divers other places of
this Realme of long time used the occupation and Crafte of Basketmaking.'[8]
The establishment of a livery company as late as this makes it suspect –
less a genuine company for the regulation of a trade than a piece of sharp
practice designed to get monopoly status for a group of entrepreneurs, a
device in which the Crown colluded because of the considerable sums paid
in duty.[9] It hardly needs saying that an occupation which the City of
London was happy to leave in the hands of the latest wave of immigrants
(mostly Huguenot refugees from the Low Countries), was not going to
present any financial threat to their English neighbours. Stow's *History of
London* (1598) says that they inhabited Pudding Lane, one of the nastier
byways, by which the butchers of Eastcheap carried the 'filth of beasts'

from the shambles to 'their dung boats on the Thames'.[10] When in 1590, in a time of dearth, the Common Council was raising 6000 quarters of wheat from the City Companies, the Basket Makers figured at the end of the list, one of 'six poore companyes we have thought necessary not to charge with any provision'.[11]

There was no 'mystery' of basket-making, and no great investment in the tools: a couple of good knives for cutting, a large bodkin for threading, a short iron bar for whacking recalcitrant withies into place, sometimes with a hole at one end called a 'governor' for straightening crooked wands, a little home-made gadget for splitting the willow-rods into three or four even strands, and the basket-maker was in business.[12]

Consequently it was a trade, even in its most regulated form, associated with poor men, and also with women workers. The 1747 survey describes the 'green' work (that is, using unpeeled withies) as requiring 'not much else besides Strength and Application, a journeyman in which can earn him 10 to 20s. a week.' The 'white work' (with peeled withies) 'does not require so much Strength, but more Invention and Nicety, at which many women are employed in making the smaller wares'.[13]

If 'not much else besides Strength and Application' was the hallmark of the trade even in London, we are justified in concluding that in the Lune Valley it was not a trade at all, but a do-it-yourself sort of occupation for dark nights and stormy weather. A recent discussion with a semi-retired fisherman of Overton, David Braid, underlined the essentially casual nature of much traditional basket-making in the area. Mr Braid still for amusement makes the 'tenels' which the Lune fishermen used for cockling, musseling, or picking up dabs and flounders, although he now uses cane, not willow. It is a skill which he learnt from his grandfather, his uncle, and his father, all fishermen, and all, as the habit was, making the baskets they needed as and when they needed them.

In Mr Braid's memory, which goes back to a time when there were ten Overton families making a living on the Lune estuary, the osiers were cut by the old men from a patch of wet ground at the edge of the village which 'belonged to the council' – common land from way back, we may believe. The 'bow' of each basket was made from hazel or wild rose cut from a hedge, because these woods are extremely whippy when green, but harden as they dry. All the baskets were made in one traditional pattern, flat, with a diamond shaped 'crown' to strengthen the join between handle and bow, but you could tell each man's work by slight differences of height, length and depth which were as good as a signature, as well as by gradations of skill. Mr Braid's uncle was a perfectionist in his selection of matching twigs – he might take two or three weeks to produce a basket that satisfied him. His father, on the other hand, made them very badly – threw one together in two or three hours, to be teased by his friends 'I see the old crow's been building another nest'. Basket-making was a bad-weather or evening occupation, the maker sitting beside the fire in the cottage, the children sitting as far as they could on the other side of the room, to dodge the stinging end of an osier carelessly pulled through and whipping their faces.

The tenels, thus made with the minimum expenditure in materials and no waste of 'working' time, were used for a season or two until they fell to pieces, and then replaced. They were strictly for use by the fishermen on the job, and not to hold the fish as it went to market. In this century at least, bags were used for that purpose, and three tenels made a bag, which caused some people to suppose that the odd word had some connection with the number three. But in fact the oyster-fishermen of Essex used a very similar basket called a 'tendle'.[14] No one in Overton village would have dreamed of giving his occupation as 'basket-maker'. Fishing was the work by which he supported himself and his family; basket-making a necessary but peripheral adjunct.

A specialist trade

In the eighteenth century, both nationally and locally, the picture begins to change towards specialisation of basket-making into an industry, though on a very small scale. Two illustrations may be quoted from that indefatigable observer, Daniel Defoe.

In his *Tour through Great Britain* (1724) Defoe refers to a proposal in which he had had a hand, 'made a few years ago to the late Lord Treasurer Godolphin' for colonising the empty spaces of the New Forest. Among the tradesmen to be needed in the new self-sufficient 'Palatinate' of six or seven hundred inhabitants, Defoe reckoned 'a hatmaker, a glover, at least two ropemakers, four taylors, three weavers of woollen, and three weavers of linnen, two basketmakers' etc. etc.[15] So basket-making to him was a specialist trade. But it is worth noting that Robinson Crusoe, driven be necessity, taught himself to make baskets with little difficulty compared with his struggles to throw a serviceable pot, and 'though not very handsome, yet they were such as were very handy and convenient for my laying things up in, or fetching things home in'.

These two examples seem to sum up the situation in the country at large: that where there was enough demand, specialists could be found to meet that demand, but the artefacts themselves were of a type which did not need the long training, the dedication, or the investment of capital of true 'mysteries' such as weaving or carpentry.

The situation in the Lune Valley seems to have followed that in the country at large. The fishermen at the mouth of the Lune were no doubt weaving their 'tenels' for their own use, but it has already been noted that in the 1730s there was a family in Caton of which two members were sufficiently certain of the importance of their trade to call themselves 'basket maker' in their marriage bonds, and Aughton also had its specialist: one John Frier at the christening of his son in 1756 is called 'wand weaver', although, as the name does not appear again, he may have been a traveller. In 1717, Ann Fenwick of Hornby paid 16*d.* a day to John Berry for seven days' basket-making. This also suggests that there was increasing demand for baskets, although one would like to know what kind of baskets and their purpose.[16]

At the same period the village of Arkholme saw the establishment of a dynasty of basket-makers called Ireland which lasted for 250 years through eight generations. From the parish records the Ireland family tree can be firmly constructed from 1700 to the present day, the family still being represented in the village, though the Ireland name died out there in 1959. Moreover, a number of its members established themselves in neighbouring places and still went on basket-making, and there is a slight suggestion that they may have been basket-makers before they arrived in Arkholme.

It cannot be absolutely proved that John Ireland, first of the line in Arkholme, whose marriage in 1700 is the first printed record of the family's long saga, was a basket-maker, but it is hard to infer anything else. Village tradition called the original John a basket-maker. In 1889 an aged member of another basket-making family, the Smiths, said that the trade had been carried on in Arkholme 'for about 200 years' and named the Irelands as the original family.[17] During John's lifetime (1674?–1751) both his sons settled in the village and raised families there, which argues for a trade rather than pure husbandry: the small Lune Valley farms could not support a father and two married sons, and in fact there is no evidence that the Irelands held land at all. In the next generation the sons of John Ireland's sons, all three of them, were definitely basket-makers. Two were called so at their marriages in 1770 and 1771, and settled in the village. The third moved across the Lune to the mother village of Melling and established the trade there.

Again there is no absolute proof, but some very clear indications, of John Ireland's arrival in Arkholme. The name was fairly widespread in Warton parish, but had not occurred previously in Arkholme, neither in the Melling parish records, nor in the extant Hearth Tax lists between 1664 and 1673, nor in the Lancashire Association Oath Rolls of 1696. These last two are lists of householders, so John Ireland did not have a father in the village. Nor did he gain settlement through his wife, as at marriage he was 'of Arkholme' but she 'of Farleton in Kendale'.

In 1674 James Ireland of Borwick had petitioned at the Quarter Sessions that as his late son John had left 'a wyfe great with Child and hath left no substance at all towards maintenance of her', that he, the 'very old, infirme and poor' father of the said John, should not also be responsible for the bastard child of his son and Jane Wilson of Arkholme.[18] The sex of the illegitimate child is not mentioned, and no baptism has yet been discovered, so its identification with John Ireland the presumed basket-maker must remain a guess, but it is a good guess. The timing is right, the name-patterns of John Ireland's children are right, his apparent landlessness and settling to a poor man's occupation also fit together; as does the fact that Jane Wilson remained in Arkholme and died there in 1719.

In fact, the Ireland tradition of basket-making may pre-date John of Arkholme. In 1739 James Ireland of Borwick, who must be a relation of the James above, and therefore presumably a relation of John of Arkholme, married and established a family at Hutton Roof. On the outside cover of his marriage bond is faintly discernible the word 'withenbounder'.[19] One explanation for two fairly remote cousins in the same trade would be that it stemmed back to a common ancestor.

A village industry: Arkholme

The Lune Valley is fertile and floods easily, so it is good osier-growing land. After floods in times past the river frequently changed its course, as can be seen on the tithe maps of the valley between Crook o' Lune and Kirkby Lonsdale. The township boundaries cross and recross the river, leaving pebbly or swampy areas which were excellent for colonisation by osiers, though the river might reclaim them in a few years after another extra high water.

It seems unlikely that osier beds were cultivated on any large scale in the eighteenth century. The tithe maps of the area offer no old field names to indicate such cultivation, except perhaps a ten-acre enclosure in Whittington called 'Witrow and Willows', but as this lies on the north side of the road to Kirkby Lonsdale, is well above river level and on a defined slope, and at the time of survey was down to arable and meadow, it would be dangerous to adduce from the name alone that it had once been used for osier plantation.

However, an unexpected source provides evidence that small patches of osiers were being cultivated, or at least enlarged and encouraged from wild beginnings. When, in 1826, evidence was being collected for the famous Hornby Castle lawsuit of *Tatham v. Wright*, neighbours of the Wright family in Aughton were being questioned, and it was said of old George Wright that he had 'two or three dales in Afton Holme a joining Lune side on some part of which grew willows … hard put to it to maintain his Famely and to pay his way … might grow a few willows at Lune side the same as other Farmers did'.

This George Wright was born in 1722 and moved to Bentham soon after 1780, so it seems that here we have a glimpse of the rather haphazard way in which the raw material of the trade was produced during the time when the first three generations of Irelands were at work. But if producing the osiers was not a full-time occupation neither, in all probability, was the basket-making. Even at the height of the Arkholme industry in the mid-nineteenth century, basket-makers were associated with all sorts of other occupations, as demand rose or fell.

Nor do we know anything about the outlets for selling their goods in the eighteenth century, although it is a good guess that the markets of Lancaster, Kirkby Lonsdale and Hornby were involved. Arkholme was a village of fewer than 300 souls, not enough to keep one basket-maker busy, let alone two or three. Agricultural commentators also point to a growing demand. Arthur Young in his *Six Months Tour through the North of England* (1770) had not a word to say on osiers or willows or even baskets, although he was very interested in various experiments in improving potato harvests. He mentions crops of 150 bushels an acre at Ormskirk, 100–200 bushels in Cockerham and Cabus, an amazing 450 bushels from a farm near Garstang. It seems very unlikely that these crops were harvested without the use of baskets, so that demand must have been growing, which is borne out by John Holt's *General View of the Agriculture of the County of Lancaster*, published 25 years later. 'The osier willow is at present in such demand for hampers &c' (the 'hamper' was an open potato basket, holding perhaps three quarters of a hundredweight) 'and there is such a scarcity of that article, that more than twenty pounds a year have been made out of a single acre of land planted with it; and though very few acres are at present planted with them, there are some thousands proper for their growth, but the management of them seems not to be understood at present'.[20] About this time the Society of Arts began to offer premiums and silver medals for the growing of basket osiers.[21]

In line with this growth in the trade, some time after 1800 osiers must

Arkholme Village Street: Although described by Nicholas Pevsner in 1969 as a 'very pretty street', these old buildings have not always been considered such desirable residences. Edwin Butterworth visiting the village in 1836 thought it 'a long street like village of mean dwellings'. (*Lancaster City Museums*)

have been planted intensively in the Lune Valley to supply the demand. In 1811 the Arkholme trade still supported only two families. The census return of that year does not name names, but does record the number of families engaged in crafts. Arkholme's tally was six: the parish register shows that there were at the time a smith, a tailor, a shoemaker and a mason in the village. That leaves two for basket-making, and these must be two grandsons of the original John: another John (1743–1826), and William (1766–1841). William's elder brother Thomas (b. 1750) had migrated to Melling, but the Arkholme families had sons, and in 1811 there may have been five men involved in the trade, which would considerably raise demand for the raw material, both in quantity and quality.

The Irelands themselves were beginning to have access to land. William Ireland was called 'basket maker' in 1802 at the christening of one child and 'farmer' two years later at the christening of another. In 1786 he had been admitted to a cottage and garden, probably at Storrs, and by the time of the tithe map survey this family had an acre of osiers along the Kirkby Lonsdale road between Storrs and Arkholme village. Three of William Ireland's sons settled to the trade, and his cousin John Ireland had acquired an interest in a small farm in 1771 by marrying a widow, Alice Cort. As the families grew they not only needed more of the raw material; they could also deploy the labour needed to grow it. It has to be remembered that this was a family craft: female and child labour could be used at several stages in the cultivation and preparation of the osiers, and sometimes in the basket-making.

The years between 1811 and 1841 show a surge in the Arkholme population, which in 1841 had topped 400, a hundred more than in either 1801 or 1901. Examination of the census returns and the parish records show that this was entirely due to the growth of the basket industry. It is perhaps significant to note that the 1831 census shows that six new houses were at that time being built in the village, and it seems likely that this period was also marked by large-scale planting of osier beds. The tithe map of 1848 shows twelve and a half acres of osiers within Arkholme township, and six and a half more across the river in Melling. Most of this, if not all, must have been intentionally planted and managed. If it were a wild infestation, one would expect to find similar growth elsewhere, but apart from two acres in Caton, which as we have seen had some tradition in basket-making, no other osier beds are shown in riverside townships between Halton and Kirkby Lonsdale.

In 1841 there were five Ireland families engaged in the trade, and four other families as well. Two were local, Smith and Taylor. The Smiths had 29 acres of their own, bordering the Lune and including most of the wild withy beds. Thomas Smith had for some reason spent time in South Wales, and tradition says he was of gypsy stock, but this seems doubtful, as he returned to take up a tenement which had been in his family time out of mind. He was always called 'yeoman' and though not wholly dependent on the craft, was the most entrepreneurial of the basket-makers. In 1841 his family of 12 included five adult children, two journeyman basket-makers, and two servants.

Two other families had come into the village more recently. John Breaks settled as a sort of hedge-schoolmaster, running a school until well into his 70s in a building which, when it was replaced in 1851, was described as 'no larger than the average kitchen'. He may have combined basket-making with the sort of undemanding school management which this suggests. His son Richard was in the trade, but had moved away before 1851. Edward Murray is an interesting newcomer: the 1851 census show that he was born in Newport in Hampshire, with a stop-off at Preston along the way to Arkholme. He was an educated man by local standards, being employed as a census enumerator in 1851. Within the nine families of 1841 there were 15 male basket-makers. Including women and children there were thus 73 people dependent on the trade, 18 per cent of the total village population.

What were they making, and where were their markets? Almost certainly agricultural baskets and hampers for the potato fields of Amounderness, which 60 years later still provided the staple trade of a much reduced output from Arkholme. Sixty years later, also, there was a sizeable trade with the Fleetwood fishing fleet, but when the Arkholme osier beds were planted, Fleetwood was only a rabbit warren on the banks of the Wyre. There may have been a demand from the growing shellfish industry of Morecambe Bay. Cockling, musseling and shrimping made a heavy demand on baskets, which were used not only for gathering but also for sending the fish to market. Several vivid descriptions exist of the employment for 12 hours a day of all the family down to children of seven and eight years,[22] and at the height of the boom, there were 45 fishing families in Bolton-le-Sands alone, before over-fishing sent the industry into decline. The gathering was very hard work but remunerative: it must have made sense to buy in at least some of the baskets they needed. One cannot be certain: the local memories which are very sure about potato hampers and Fleetwood baskets have never heard of a connection with Morecambe Bay.

The same transport developments which opened up the Morecambe Bay fisheries were there for exploitation by the basket-makers also. The Preston canal was opened in 1797 and extended to Kendal in 1821. It passed through Borwick, about four miles from Arkholme. In the 1840s the railway linked Lancaster with Preston and the manufacturing towns of south Lancashire. In 1846 it was completed to Carlisle. We can only guess at the effect of these developments; until the very end of the nineteenth century, a period that living memories can just reach back to, Lune Valley basket-making remained 'an inferior Hidden Sort of Handicraft Business'.

The First World War brought home to people how much rural life and rural industries were changing and vanishing, leaving no records. To survive village crafts had to move with the industrial times or go under. Although they were hand crafts, they had somehow to find a niche in the steam-driven new world. Their raw materials, output and distribution needed management and entrepreneurial skill to survive, even before the arrival of cheap imports which is often blamed exclusively for the decay of hand crafts.

In the Oxford area the plight of the very small craftsman was described: 'It appears that the poverty and depression of these men is partly due to lack of skill; instead of serving a thorough apprenticeship, they have picked up from their fathers possibly one kind of basket only, depression and insufficient livelihood have reacted on their work, and the decline of local osier-growing and lack of means to acquire land for beds of their own, has put them at a disadvantage ... Hence they use poor material and turn out poor work.' [23]

In 1922 there was published a very thorough survey of the osier-growing and basket-making industries.[24] At that time the Trent Valley, Somerset, and Mawdesley in Lancashire were the most important areas for growing osiers, accounting for about 2000 acres, but the very size of these operations make them of doubtful value in interpreting what actually happened in smaller places.

If we describe best practice: the rods were planted at between 15000 and 24000 to the acre, the easiest part of osier growing being that a slip of the wood will always grow if pushed in the ground. The fields, or holts, had to be kept extremely clean by a mixture of hand weeding and horse-hoeing, particularly in the first year, when the infant rods were weeded four times. The first year's growth had to be cut, but was not of much use to the industry. The cutting, by a sharp blade very close to the point of growth, was a skilled operation. Careless cutting caused the residual gnarled growth of wood, or 'stool', to become too high above the ground; really skilled cutting kept the stools so low that after harvesting there was little to be seen but a sort of flat wooden plate from which next year's shoots would start.

The cut rods had to be harvested, sorted into sizes, dried with the bark on for 'brown' work, peeled while the sap was still rising for 'white' work. Those were the two original colours, but in the 1860s a third option was introduced, boiling the rods, originally in urine but later in water, for anything up to 12 hours, and peeling them while they were still hot, which gave them a distinctive tan or 'buff' colour. The rods were split lengthwise into three or four, and then had to be damped again to keep them flexible when the basket-maker actually wanted to work with them.

The survey quoted above described best practice but found many poorly kept beds and ignorant growers. A well-kept holt would produce after four years, go on for ten, and with care might be kept going for thirty. Then it ought to be completely grubbed up, put down to grass for four or five years, and started over again. Poor practice resulted in only the worst stumps being grubbed up and another rod put back in the gap to grow again, usually an overlong rod which would not be choked by the surrounding mature stools.

The surveyors found, not unexpectedly, that where basket-makers owned their own osier beds they looked after them better than did farmers who simply filled up unwanted corners of land and sold the crop. Weedy, waterlogged, or neglected beds made the willows liable to blight by weakening the stocks.

The pattern of rise and fall of the Arkholme industry suggests that poor management of the osier beds was a large part of the trouble, although some of it may have been due to river floods. Contrary to popular belief, fine osiers do not grow well on swampy ground, although they like a high water table.

In 1848, we have seen, there were 19 acres under osier cultivation in Arkholme and Melling, but it is clear from the tithe map schedule that these acres were neither owned nor leased by the basket-makers. Apart from a small plot previously mentioned as belonging to one of the Ireland families, and some insignificant growth on the Smiths' land, these beds were part of various larger farms. Who worked them, or how well they were worked, is not known. It seems certain that the basket-makers cut the osiers and brought them back to their workshops, because the oral tradition is that they did this, and there are one or two late nineteenth-century photographs. But there is no tradition of the beds being cared for, or managed, or replaced, to any significant degree. Towards the end of the century the largest local land-owner, Francis Pearson of Storrs, planted, or allowed to be planted, small new beds on unwanted corners of his land, which indicates that by that time most of the original plantations had been cleared for grazing or had reverted to the wild.

By 1851 the industry in Arkholme had started its long slow decline, which fits with a scenario of enthusiastic large-scale planting in the 1830s unaccompanied by any real understanding of the management of the beds. In 1851 there were 14 basket-makers, supporting 46 people, or 14 per cent of the population. In 1861 the figures were much the same, the families still Ireland, Taylor, Smith and Murray (five Irelands to one each of the others). However, by 1871 there were only seven basket-makers, supporting six per cent of the population, and this in spite of the fact that the branch railway through Arkholme, connecting with the west coast network at Carnforth, and in the other direction with Leeds and Bradford, had opened in 1868 and four trains were scheduled in each direction each day. Basket-making remained a poor livelihood eked out with other jobs. At different times Irelands in Arkholme kept a grocery shop and post office, mended boots, ran the Melling ferry, and did a bit of smallholding.

For many generations the Irelands carried their family craft with them even in dispersal. By 1851 an Ireland had settled in Stonewell, Lancaster, and continued his trade there. The 1866 Street Directory shows another in Morecambe, no doubt making fish baskets. In 1881 the Stonewell family was still going in the second generation and two more Irelands were working in Skerton. As late as 1954 there was a very old Roger Ireland working at Lansil in Lancaster, making wicker covers for carboys.

Potato-hampers and carboy covers were at the rough end of the craft, but the last of the Irelands, Charlie, who died in 1959, was a different sort of workman, a skilled craftsman who largely abandoned the rough trade and concentrated on bicycle- and flower-baskets, neat clothes hampers and other fancy goods. Although he grew a few osiers, experimenting with different types, in the patch of ground behind his house in Arkholme, 'Willow Cottage', and although his nephew remembers going with him to cut rough willows from the sewage farms at Burton and Bentham and Ingleton, he imported the finer rods from a Manchester dealer for most of his work. These may well have come from the Mawdesley fields, where the fine 'Dicky Meadowes' were grown, osiers, it was said, whose nature was so kind that 'you could have laced your boots with them'.

It has to remain a puzzle how, given that he learnt the trade from his father who had a reputation as a very rough workman, making nothing but potato hampers, Charlie acquired such skill, nor is it clear where he found the patterns for his artefacts. Perhaps the catalogues from which he selected his raw materials also had illustrations of finished articles, perhaps customers brought him old things to copy, or drew sketches, and his undoubted artistry did the rest. As he is the only local basket-maker now remembered, his high level of achievement has coloured the folk-memory of the whole industry.

Charlie's work was always in demand locally, and towards Christmas he worked nearly 20 hours a day to fill orders. But it was not enough. He seems not to have had even the every simple machines which lightened the tasks of peeling and splitting, although the imported rods were probably already peeled and split. The old cast-iron boiler was constantly in need of patching with a home-made cement of cowdung and straw, and he had no form of transport: his customers simply came to the door. Because he was a fine craftsman they came, and the boost in demand due to the Second World War enabled him to make a living. But the time was past for the single village craftsman making useful everyday artefacts at an affordable price. Charlie Ireland's death in 1959 marked the end of the Lune Valley osier basket-makers.

Burton's wand-weavers

An unusual later extension of the basket-maker's trade was found in Burton in Lonsdale, where Irelands and Taylors from Arkholme were prominent in the workforce. The pottery industry of Burton was already long-established in 1767, when the Enclosure Act reserved to the inhabitants of Bentham and Burton in perpetuity certain clay strata on Bentham Moor.[25] Below the layer which was used for the local 'blackware' was another suitable for stoneware and firebricks. This began to be exploited

Burton Basket Makers: The repetitive nature of this craft can be appreciated simply by considering the rows of jars requiring identical baskets which are pictured in these photos (*Lancaster City Musuems*/Henry Bateson)

in 1835. New potteries were started to deal with it, and once the railway network allowed of their export, the stoneware bottles were being sent in large numbers to Liverpool, Ireland and the Isle of Man. These bottles, particularly those destined for the distillers of 'ardent spirits' were protected by wicker covers, and once again the census returns show how the trade developed. In 1841 there was one basket-maker, who may have been a general tradesman, since the 1851 census shows none. In 1861 there were two, one of them an Ireland from Arkholme. In 1871 there were seven and in 1881 eight, three of whom were born in Arkholme, including an Ireland and a Taylor. One basket-maker kept the 'Penny Bridge'. At the height of the Burton trade there were 15 kilns in Burton, turning out both their domestic country pottery, and the stoneware bottles in every size from a pint to five gallons. The last closed in 1945.

Wray's swill-makers

Also at about the time of the end of the Arkholme industry, a much shorter-lived operation also came to an end, across the river in Wray. This was the making of oak spale baskets or swills.

Since the eighteenth century Wray was an industrial village, with hatters' and nailers' workshops, and at various times coal mining and quarrying. There was one large source of employment in the form of the mill which, probably because of the uncertainty of the water flow from the Roeburn, was constantly going out of business and starting up again.[26] And at Millhouses (actually in Tatham township but effectively part of Wray) was another mill on the Hindburn, which had once been the corn mill of the Manor of Tatham, but which in the nineteenth century served various timber trades.

A stray receipted bill of July 1890 shows that William Fleming, 'wisket manufacturer' (another name for swills) was operating from Millhouses, and that he had recently moved from Nibthwaite.[27] This was an industry much followed in parts of North Lonsdale and Westmorland, where the oak woods were coppiced for the trade, the peeled bark going to the tanneries, and the logs cut into suitable lengths and then split and split again into ever finer thicknesses, from which the wiskets were woven.

There is no evidence as to why William Fleming chose Wray: there was some suitable oak coppice at hand though not to be compared with the Lake District; there was the sawmill; there were people who understood something of woods and timber work, and it seems likely that there was a good supply of labour and houses. The mill on the Roeburn had also just gone into liquidation yet again, as the 1891 census shows a full third of the houses in Wray standing empty.

The same year, 1891, saw the arrival of the family with which swill-making was to be associated for the rest of its existence – the Singletons. There were three Singletons: John I (d. 1941), John II (1883–1965), John III (1909–1991). Their history is patchy, largely a matter of family tradition. John I is said to have been a Cumbrian man, who spent time at Gargunnock near Stirling, and came south again during the 1880s, living for a short

Oak Swill Makers, Wray in the early twentieth century: From left to right: John Singleton II, John Singleton I, Thomas Bevins. John Singleton III carried on the trade for some time after the Second World War but Dick Bevins, the son of Thomas, who married the sister of John II, was the last swill maker in the village, only giving up the trade in the later 1960s. (Photo courtesy of Judy Wilson)

time at Bouth before finally settling at Wray. A few photographs remain, and an order book covering the years between 1923 and 1956, at which date the Singleton's business ended. There is also a letter from John Singleton II in the archives of the Library of the Rural History Centre at Reading, written in 1961. He was a literate man, for 50 years Clerk to Wray Parish Council, and it would seem that he had been asked to describe a dying craft. It was dying like the osier-weaving trade, although in 1952 60 families could still be found earning their living by it in the Furness district.[28]

The swills were made in various sizes, usually 20, 24 or 26 inches. Flexible hazel or ash sticks made the oval rim. The oak logs for riving had to be carefully chosen and cut in the woods. They were seasoned for several months and then very thoroughly boiled and soaked. Splitting or riving began with an axe, and ended with a knife and the workman's hands. This part of the work was at least as skilled as the weaving. Each man, wearing kneepads for protection, dipped into the boiling water for the softened wood and rived it into 'spales' or 'spells' (shorter pieces used side to side) and 'tars' (longer pieces used end to end). On Monday he made a pile of riven oak and of hazel 'bools' (the basket rims) to last him until Friday. Thirty baskets was the tally for the week, but a good workman could make 36; Saturday morning was spent preparing the oak logs for Monday's boiling. A well-made swill would hold water.

Oak swills were in immense demand on farms, in bobbin and other mills, and not least for coaling ships. White Star Line, it is said, issued contracts for 1000 dozen at a time. The Singletons' order book only gives the names of recipients, and it is not always possible to say what use would finally be made of the goods, but a number of customers were in the North East, in Stockton, Darlington, and Bishop Auckland, and others nearer home, in Lancaster or Settle. Among them were bobbin mills, greengrocers, market gardeners, ironmongers, agricultural implement dealers, and the brickworks at Claughton. John II mentions Scottish farmers' supply merchants ordering by the 100 dozen, a 22 inch basket holding approximately three stone of potatoes. Other private customers bought one or two at a time for their gardens. The big orders tended to come in the autumn and the Singletons would build up a supply of two or three hundred dozen over the summer. The largest number shown for a year in the order book is 354 dozen in 1937.

It was always a small business, though it is said that at its height it employed seven people. John I was something of a wanderer, who liked to 'go on a spree'. He did the woodland work. John II was a steady worker who is remembered as never leaving the workshop, though in the spring, when the chosen trees were barked, all hands had to turn to that job, which had to be done without delay, while the sap was rising. The bark was a profitable sideline – it was chopped up and sold to the tanneries. When John II wrote his letter in 1961 he was 77 years old and retired. He said that his son had 'gone out of the business ... because of the lack of foresters who can exploit coppice'. John III went out of the trade and worked for the council, but in his retirement he was tempted back to do some demonstration work, and to pass on some of his skill to one or two young people who can still turn their hand to the craft.

Swill-making died out with the retirement in the late 1960s of the last full-time craftsman in Wray, Dick Bevins. He was the son of Thomas Bevins who had trained under the Singletons and had married John II's sister. Jessica Lofthouse painted an appealing picture of his 'sunlit workshop' in one of her travelogues. 'I sat on a bench swept clean of shavings and was initiated into the old craft. There was a delicious scent, a blending of sweet apples, lemons and pines, yet the swill-maker could smell nothing. His nose had become used to it.' When she suggested that if his secluded workshop opened into the main street he 'would be as great an attraction as the blacksmith with his smithy under Longfellow's spreading chestnut tree', he replied simply that 'he was glad enough to be spared all that publicity'.[29] Family and local tradition maintains that he recognised swill-making for what it was, a necessary means to earn a living, but that he would much have preferred to have spent his time walking the hills he loved.

The modern oak swill is useful, attractive, and expensive. A good many people in the Lune Valley, who have pleasure in handmade artefacts, gather their garden weeds or store their logs in a genuine swill made in the last

Oak Swill Makers: Thomas Bevins (left) and Dick (right) at work outside the family's workshop which was located in the garden behind their house on Wray Main Street. (Photos courtesy of Judy Wilson and David Kenyon)

20 years, but this is a craft, not an industry. The industry has gone, and will not come back.

Notes

I am grateful for help and information given me by Nigel Dalziel of the Lancaster Maritime Museum, Stan Lawrence (on the Burton-in-Lonsdale trades), Rose Pierce, David Braid, Stella Kenyon, Susan Pearson, Alan Webster, Robert Bassenden and Pat Livermore.

1.   G. Fransson, *Mediaeval Surnames of Occupation* (1935).
2.   T. Waller, *A General Description of All Trades* (1747).
3.   Lancashire Parish Register Society, Vols 1–139, 1897–1996.
4.   Record Society of Lancashire and Cheshire, Vols 74, 75, 115.
5.   LRO, DDGa 18, A Copy of All Men's Names ... in the Hundred of Lonsdale ... Between the Ages of 18 and 50 Years.
6.   LRO, WRW (L) and WRW (K). Probate Records, Richmond Deanery (Lonsdale and Kendal).
7.   H. H. Bobart, *Records of the Basket-makers' Company* (1911), p. 6.
8.   Bobart, *Records*, p. 32
9.   Bobart, *Records*, p. 2.
10. John Stow, *History of London* (Everyman edn., 1945), p. 189.
11. Bobart, *Records*, p. 75.
12. A. Heseltine, *Baskets and Basketmaking* (1982), p. 14.
13. Waller, *Description*, quoted in Bobart, *Records*, p. 147.
14. Dorothy Wright, *The Complete Book of Baskets and Basketry* (1977), p. 151.
15. Daniel Defoe, *Tour Through Great Britain* (Folio Society edition, 1983), Vol. I, p. 221.
16. LRO, RCHy 2/4/30. I am grateful to Jennifer Holt for giving me this reference
17. *Lancaster Gazette*, July 1889.
18. LRO, QSP 414/13.
19. I am grateful to Pat Livermore of Scotforth for this discovery.
20. John Holt, *General View of the Agriculture of the County of Lancaster* (1795, reprint David & Charles, 1965), p. 85.
21. Dorothy Wright, Article in *Good Work*, Vol. 28, No. 1, 1965.
22. K. Entwistle, *From Bodeltune to Bolton-le-Sands* (1982).
23. K. S. Woods, *Rural Industries Round Oxford* (1921), p. 116.
24. H. E. FitzRandolph & M. D. Hay, *Rural Industries of England and Wales* (Oxford, 1926), Vol. II, pp. 3–88.
25. *Lancaster Guardian*, 4 September 1875.
26. *Lancaster Guardian*, 16 March 1889, 'Wray: The Decayed Industries of the Village'. See also *Lancaster Guardian*, 27 July 1934.
27. Material in the possession of Stella Kenyon of Wray, who kindly lent it to me.
28. *Country Life*, 4 January 1952.
29. Information from Judith Wilson of Farleton (Thomas Bevins' granddaughter) and David Kenyon of Wray. J. Lofthouse, *Lancashire's Fair Face – Discoveries Ribble to Lune* (London, 1952), pp. 184–5.

CHAPTER SIX

The Hat Industry

Christine Workman

Felt hat-making became an important, workshop-based industry in the Lune Valley in the eighteenth and early nineteenth centuries. It developed on the back of the domestic 'consumer revolution' generated by rising living standards and an increasing population at this time, and by the close proximity of the port of Lancaster and its burgeoning overseas trade. Hatting was established first as one of Lancaster's many trades, then as part of a dual economy in the rural areas immediately to the east of the town, notably the parish of Quernmore and the township of Over Wyresdale, and ultimately as a specialised centre of production, especially in the village of Wray, where felt hats were produced for well over a hundred years.

The hat trade in Britain before 1800

Tradition has it that the felt hat was invented in 1456 and first made in London in 1510, though some form of knitted felt hat had probably been made earlier.[1] The Feltmakers' Company emerged to govern the trade in the seventeenth century. Its first charter was in 1604 although a dispute with the Merchant Haberdashers, representatives of the Hatters and Cappers, who were opposed to the felt makers as they rightly feared for their livelihood, meant that a full charter was not granted till 1667. The first felt hatters, exiled Huguenots from France, set up their businesses in Southwark and Bermondsey in London and this area remained a major centre of hat production until the late nineteenth century. However, increasing demand, in terms of both number and style of hats, from the early seventeenth century led to increasing production in these parts of London, but also to areas in and around the major provincial towns of Chester, Manchester, Kendal and Bristol which were near domestic supplies of wool.[2]

Between 1680 and about 1740 there was an unparalleled growth in hat production in London, based mainly on the export of fashionable Beaver hats to markets in Europe, particularly Spain, Portugal and their colonies, but also with British North American colonies. Annual exports peaked in 1736 at 700,000 hats. However, output of Beaver hats stagnated between 1750 and 1770, partly due to competition from French producers, partly due to the overtrapping of beavers in North America. At the same time, felt hat production began to increase, and spiralling labour costs in London led metropolitan hatters to seek alternative, cheaper sources of labour, raw materials and forms of production. Attention switched to the provincial centres with their coarse felts for the domestic market and considerably cheaper labour costs. Initially London hatters subcontracted work to provincial masters who made up raw material that they sent to them, but eventually they set up their own branches. The area around Stockport and towns to the north of Manchester became the centre of a thriving Cheshire/Lancashire provincial trade. As early as 1751 Richard and Francis Crofton of London had an agreement with Samuel Edgley of Manchester to make hats with material supplied by them. Other London manufacturers set up their own provincial base, such as Thomas Davies in Stockport in 1761. As a result, felt hats took over from Beavers in the export trade. Demand was further boosted from the 1770s by the British army who wore them in campaigns in Spain and America. By 1800 over one and a quarter million felt hats were exported per annum.[3]

By this time, many different styles of felt hat were made in England. The main choice was between the cocked hat, used for ceremonial or formal occasions, and the top hat, with fashion dictating the height of the crown and whether it was tapered, conical or concave in shape. Likewise, the brim changed in width and form. Colours varied, mainly black (dyed using logwood) or drab (natural colour) but also white (from white rabbit fur), beige or brown were common. Price varied accordingly. In the late eighteenth century the 'square' or 'taper' crowns were 8s. a dozen and by 1824 had increased to 10s. per dozen to manufacture.[4]

This increasing and diversifying national and international demand served to further boost specialist provincial centres of production. This, coupled with the development of Lancaster as an Atlantic port, were major factors in the growth of the local hatting industry around this time. It is not known when the trade first began in the Lune Valley, but the earliest known reference to a hatter dates from 1674 when James Bancroft of Lancaster bought wool from Sarah Fell of Swarthmoor Hall and, in return, sold Quaker hats to her.[5] As demand increased, expansion took place first in Lancaster, the oldest local centre of production, but then spread to rural locations in Over Wyresdale and Quernmore as part of a dual farming economy, and then as a full-time trade to industrial settlements such as Wray and Bentham. However, the development of the trade cannot be fully appreciated without first examining the processes involved in the making of a felt hat.

The art of hat-making

The manufacture of a felt hat involved three separate stages: the preparation of the raw materials; the making of the hat base and finishing.[6] It was a dirty trade in which men worked in poor conditions and in temperatures that oscillated between hot to cold depending on the stage of the felting process. The processes involved remained virtually unchanged until the industry was mechanised relatively late in the mid-nineteenth century.

A variety of raw materials was used depending on the type of hat required. James Bancroft, for example, used the wool from Sarah Fell's own sheep to make her Quaker hats. However, the best wool, Merino, was imported from Germany and Spain.'Stuff hats' were made with a mixture of wool and fur. In the eighteenth century imported beaver fur led to the fashionable 'Beaver hat', but increasing scarcity meant that it became an expensive commodity. By the early nineteenth century most such hats were 'plated', i.e. a fine finish of fur was applied on to a basic wool body, and the term 'Beaver hat' was increasingly given to the style of hat rather than to its major ingredient. There is no evidence, however, that hats plated with beaver and other furs such as nutria, seal and camel were made locally. The functional felt hats or hat bodies made in the Lune Valley relied primarily on more common wild rabbit fur and relatively cheap wool.

First the fleece was sorted and the shorter fibres, which were amenable to felting were selected. The wool was then carded.[7] This was probably done at home, possibly by women, although wool for the Wray hatters might have been carded at Wray mill. Rabbit fur was shorn off the skin and 'carrotted', a process in which the fur was treated with mercuric nitrate to render the fibres suitable for the felting process in which it was blended with the wool. The phrase, 'as mad as a hatter' refers to the shakes which a hatter could develop from mercuric poisoning. There is no evidence that this was a major problem in the Lune Valley, although it is possibly significant that a number of hatters were admitted to the County Lunatic Asylum in Lancaster in the early nineteenth century.[8]

The actual making of the hat was a male occupation carried out in a workshop, which was often nothing more than a converted barn or outbuilding. Hats were made according to their weight and the 'ingredients' were weighed out in proportion of wool to other fur. The first part of the process was called 'bowing'. It took place in a draughtless area on a workbench which was often made from wicker to allow dirt and dust generated in the process to fall through the cracks to the floor.

Bowing: 'The material being spread on the board, the bow is drawn down nearly on the table, the middle of its frame being held firmly in the workman's left hand, the string being now almost on a level with the wool is drawn out with the right hand, and when allowed to recoil, it strikes the wool, and separates and mixes its fibres; which, after floating for a time in the air, gently descend, and lie in a loose flock, on the surface of the board.' (*Saturday Magazine*, 10 January 1835)

Suspended from the ceiling was a bow about five feet long with a catgut string which the hatter twanged over the fur and wool with a wooden pin. This caused the wool and fur to fly into the air and to float down to form a loose mat of overlapping fibres. This mat was then formed into a triangular shape with the material being slightly thicker where the brim and the crown were to be formed. The material was then compressed by placing a piece of leather over it and applying pressure. Water was applied to assist adhesion. Two of these 'pads' were next combined to form the basic hat shape. A piece of stiff paper of the same triangular shape as the matted fibre mat, but somewhat smaller, was laid on each pad, and the edges of the pad folded over. Two pads were then superimposed and the whole sprinkled with water and rolled to unite the fibres into a conical shape. The paper was then removed and the roughly-formed conical hat body taken to the 'battery'.

This next stage of the process was felting, or planking as it was sometimes known. This was the most important part of the manufacturing process which determined the waterproof finish and quality of the hat. The 'battery' consisted of a circular copper or iron kettle with six or eight mahogany planks angled into it, each of which provided a working surface for a hatter. The kettle was filled with very hot water and sulphuric acid which was heated by a turf or coal fire beneath. The conical hat was continually dipped in this liquid and then rolled on the planks until the material had shrunk and adhered to form a felt. When the body had been reduced to the required dimensions it was removed and allowed to dry. It was then waterproofed with shellac or other resins and gums. If the hat was to be plated with beaver or other fur, it was applied at this stage and returned to the kettle for further manipulation to adhere the beaver fibres to the hat body. The plating and finishing of a beaver hat, however, was a skilled job and the felt bodies produced locally for fashionable hats were probably sent to London to be finished since country hatters were generally regarded as inferior to skilled metropolitan artisans. However, the simpler styled felt hats for the export trade were made and finished locally.

The newly formed conical hat was then wetted and placed on a wooden block or mould and pulled down to produce the required crown hat shape and size. The excess felt at the bottom of the mould was used to form the brim. It was then dipped in cold water to stiffen it by hardening the varnish. The final stages involved dyeing and finishing which could be done either in the workshop or at specialist dyers. The hats were clipped and then rubbed with pumice to remove the coarse nap and then carded with a fine card before being dyed in a copper vat with a mixture of logwood and copper and iron mordants such as verdigris and copperas to make the dye fast.[9] Irons were then used to smooth the surface and give it a good gloss.[10] The final trimming and lining may have been done by women in the home or in a workshop but away from the planking shop.

Hatters, therefore, required relatively few tools – cards for the wool,

The Hatmakers' Battery: 'This battery consists of a metal vessel, called the kettle, in the centre, surrounded by six or eight inclined wooden planes; the liquid in the kettle is kept nearly boiling, by means of a flue that runs round it, connected with a furnace.' (*Saturday Magazine*, 10 January 1835.) This illustration depicts several different stages of hat production which would have taken place around the kettle.

shears or scissors to trim the fur and the finished hats, a bow, a kettle, a wooden rolling pin, wooden or stone moulds probably made by local blockmakers, and irons for finishing. Often they are referred to in inventories as hatters' tools and only the kettle, the major financial outlay, is specified individually. Adequate supplies of turf or coal, and easy access to water were important, but the location of a workshop was not dictated by the external sources of power. A master hatter could own or rent a workshop and employ journeymen and no more than two apprentices if he abided by Guild and, later, union regulations. Investment in buildings was modest, varying from retail outlets in Lancaster to converted barns in rural areas and a purpose-built workshop in Wray.

Lancaster

Local production was initially centred on Lancaster. Its importance grew during the eighteenth century and then contracted. Manufacturing was also closely connected with men who were involved in trade, either as retailers or merchants. Some idea of the possible extent and nature of the industry can be gauged from the freeman rolls (extant from 1709) and apprentice lists, since trading in Lancaster was restricted to freemen and those who paid a fine which was entered on the stallenge roll. Early references to the trade refer to both feltmakers and hatters and the terms are interchangeable to a large extent. George Mann is the first hatter listed in 1709–10.[11] From then until 1750 eleven hatters became freemen, but numbers more than doubled to 28 between 1751 and 1800. The peak year was 1801–2 when seven hatters were admitted as freemen. Thereafter numbers declined and William Blacow, son of James Blacow, a hatter, who had been made a freeman in 1811–12 is the last entry in 1830–31, although it is known that the hatting trade continued on a smaller scale in Lancaster till the late nineteenth century. Hatting apprentices in the eighteenth century in Lancaster show a similar pattern to that of the number of freemen hatters. Between 1708 and 1799, 45 apprentice hatters or feltmakers were bound in Lancaster to fifteen master craftsmen.[12] A significant minority of these are known to have come from farming backgrounds, indicative of growing rural-urban migration at the time as well as the desire to learn a trade which was seen as a superior occupation to that of a mere husbandman.

These increases reflect not just the growing domestic demand for hats (at that time, virtually everyone wore a hat), but also coincides with the period of rapid expansion in Lancaster's lucrative overseas trade between the 1740s and early 1800s, most notably to the Americas, West Indies and the West African slave coast.[13] The hatters sold their products to local merchants who bought a range of other goods from manufacturers as far away as Manchester, as well as from Lancaster and its hinterland, for export. Hats were part of their staple general trade but were also specifically exported for sale to the plantation owners for their slaves who required basic, hard wearing hats, so-called 'negro hats', to protect them from the tropical sun.[14]

The involvement of local Quakers in this overseas trade is particularly well documented. As high office was denied to them they often turned to what were considered to be respectable trades and commerce. They met at the Lancaster Meeting House for their monthly meeting and were able to set up trade links through their considerable communication network with other Quakers throughout the country. Their great influence can be seen throughout the history of the local hat trade, in both Lancaster and surrounding rural areas. Among the earliest examples of Quaker merchants exporting hats was Joshua Lawson who sent four dozen felt hats on the *Imployment* to Virginia in 1698.[15] In 1724 Robert Lawson Jr. sent 93 dozen felt hats and 104 dozen woollen caps to Jamaica and the following year Robert Lawson & Co. sent 400 dozen felt hats and 200 dozen woollen caps on the *Love* bound for Antigua.[16] Other Quakers, such as Benjamin Satterthwaite, represented the merchants' interests in the West Indies in the 1740s, selling felt hats among a range of goods.[17] The Lawsons and the Dilworth-Rawlinson merchant group, who became increasingly active from the 1730s, were particularly successful and gradually became dominant by the end of the century.[18]

The growth in the local hat trade reflected the considerable increase in hat exports for the whole of the United Kingdom between 1700 and 1760. Evidence on the precise extent of the trade is elusive, but there are more examples of it by the 1780s. In 1785 the Rawlinsons sent the *Cavendish* to the Windward Islands. Her cargo included 14 dozen assorted hats from Joseph Atkinson of Manchester, and an assortment of hats from various

Lancaster hatters: 40 dozen men's bound hats @ 11s. 6d. per dozen from John Scales; 40 dozen hats @ 11s. per dozen from Christopher She(a)rson; 40 dozen bound men's hats from George Braithwaite; and 30 dozen seamen's bound felt hats from William Braithwaite.[19] Not surprisingly, this trade enriched many local hatters. Christopher Sherson, for example, had been one of four apprentices of William Scales between 1748 and 1755. He was made a Freeman in 1763 and himself took eight apprentices between 1767 and 1795. In 1809 his estate was valued at £5000.[20] His son, John, carried on the trade. Likewise, John Scales, William's son, took six apprentices between 1776 and 1797.

However, Lancaster's foreign trade peaked around 1800 and then de-clined, exacerbated by French Revolutionary and Napoleonic Wars, French privateers and economic depression after 1815. The port's inability to accommodate larger vessels, competition from other ports, particularly Liverpool, and the decline of the West Indies sugar trade after 1800 were also important factors. This decline in overseas trade is mirrored in the decline of hatting and other Lancaster trades which had prospered because of it but it also reflects a decline of the felt hat trade nationally which accelerated in the 1830s and 1840s. When national trade recovered in the 1850s, it was increasingly concentrated in fewer centres and the local trade did not revive.

Quernmore and Over Wyresdale

Eighteenth-century growth was not restricted to Lancaster. The establish-ment of workshops in Quernmore and Over Wyresdale can be seen as a local manifestation of the national trend to set up in rural locations outside the influence of the restrictive guilds where masters were free to organise labour as they pleased and as the seasons dictated. It also reflected the expansion of manufacturing as a secondary occupation into areas of predominately pastoral farming which required less labour and in which there were times in the year when there was little work to do on the land.[21] Locally, the port of Lancaster and the growth of its overseas trade clearly offered considerable potential. There was also a plentiful supply of raw materials.

Unlike Lancaster, the industry in this rural district was characterised by single workshops, often converted barns, sometimes isolated but more usually adjacent to a farm and consequently part of a dual economy. Hat workshops are known to have been associated with farms at Brow Top, Gibsons, Greenalls and Rowton Brook (Quernmore); Moor Head in Over Wyresdale, where it may have developed from the local linen and woollen cottage industries which were evident in the seventeenth and eighteenth centuries; and the hamlet of Tarnbrook, where the Townleys and Gornalls plied their trade in the eighteenth and early nineteenth centuries.[22]

The earliest documented hatter in Quernmore is William Birkett, whose estate was valued at £152 on his death in 1726, although it is not known where he worked. His will indicated that he knew William Stout of Lancaster, suggesting possible trade links with the local merchant.[23] A major hatting shop at Greenalls was probably being worked as early as the 1730s and was associated with the Gibson and Greenall families from at least 1766 until 1815. Francis Gibson, a hatter in 1726, was made a freeman in 1735–6. It is not known when he purchased Gibsons but he had definitely acquired Greenalls by 1766, when it was occupied by his brother-in-law and nephew, John and Richard Greenall, who were also hatters.[24] This close-knit hatting community also included Gibson's brother, John, and two other nephews, John and James Greenall. Only one kettle is mentioned, so their shop probably employed eight men at most. The presence of 20 stones of wool and hat linings to the combined value of £10 16s. 0d. in Francis Gibson's inventory of 1769 supports the view that the Quernmore hatters made stiff woollen hats.[25] It is difficult to assess the relative importance of hatting and agriculture in their dual economy. Both Gibson and Greenall kept animals and possessed husbandry gear but described themselves as hatters.

The hat trade must have been very profitable in the 1760s as debts due to John Greenall on his death in 1767 amounted to £322 19s. 8d. and his inventory was valued at £129 11s. 6d.[26] Two years later Francis Gibson's estate, including animals and husbandry gear, was worth £126 4s. 6d. and he had £200 invested in trade. As both men were freemen of Lancaster, it is reasonable to assume that they were also involved in some way with overseas trade. This hat shop must have continued to be profitable at least until 1807 as Richard Greenall, Gibson's nephew, had been able to loan £600 to his brother. It was still a hat workshop in 1836.[27]

The Quaker influence on the hat trade in Quernmore centred on the Mason family, who are known to have been located at Rowton Brook. George Mason was a linen weaver who had moved from Dent. He married twice with a substantial issue. Three sons entered the hat trade. George resided at Rowton Brook farm, while Thomas and John lived in Wray, the latter being an important figure in the development of the trade there. Thomas, a grandson, married Ellen Thompson, daughter of a hat manufacturer and they continued to live at Rowton Brook in the early nineteenth century.[28] Interestingly, this farm and Hare Apple Tree, which is also reputed to have hatting associations, are located at the foot of Clougha Fell and are linked by footpaths to the hatters of Moor Head in Wyresdale.

Over Wyresdale was also a Quaker stronghold and the hat trade here was dominated by them. Moor Head Estate consisted of several tenements occupied in the early eighteenth century by the Dilworth, Townson, Procter and Birkett families, all Quakers. The hat factory at Higher Moor Head farm associated with the Birkett and Procter families was a two storey, free-standing barn with flues for two kettles. Members of both families are known to have traded as freemen in Lancaster. William

Birkett, like Francis Gibson, was made a freeman in 1735 and James Procter in 1759. The Birketts continued the hatting trade at Moor Head until the late 1830s. They are known to have sold hats to the Rawlinsons whose ship manifests show that William Birkett's grandsons, William and Richard Birkett, sent 40 dozen hats @ 9s. 6d. per dozen to Jamaica in 1786 on the *Two Brothers*. Richard Birkett also sent 30 dozen coarse woollen hats on the same ship two years earlier. There may well have been a formal partnership with the Procter family. In 1792 Thomas Procter was described as a master hatter at Higher Moor Head, employing '7 or 8 men constantly' including his son, William, who in 1798 married Sarah, the daughter of William Birkett who then resided at Lower Moor Head.[29] Thomas Procter sent 38 dozen men's hats bound with black on the *Active* bound for Jamaica in 1785. Both William Birkett and Thomas Procter were also farmers. When William died in 1815, aged 72, his estate was valued at £450. He left his share of the 'Hatting Utencils, Hats Woolle' valued at £25 to his eldest son, William. He had cattle valued at £92, yet he called himself a hat manufacturer. Interestingly, while most hatters signed their wills, William Birkett made his mark.[30]

It is difficult to estimate how many other hatters worked in Over Wyresdale and Quernmore between the 1730s and 1830s. Numerous hatters appear in the parish registers, but it is impossible to locate them precisely within the district. Nor is it possible to identify precisely how many master craftsmen there were. The Townley brothers and Thomas Gornall, for example, are known to have been country masters in Tarnbrook, but whether they worked together or each had a workshop is not clear.[31] They were certainly closely connected. Gornall's apprenticeship to John Morley, a master hatter known to have been working in Upper Wyresdale in 1787, had been witnessed by John Townley of Tarnbrook.[32]

Old Hat Factory, Higher Moor Head Farm, Wyresdale, 1997: A two storey, free-standing barn with flues for two kettles. This workshop was associated with the Birkett and Procter families in the eighteenth century. The Birketts continued the hatting trade at Moor Head until the late 1830s. (Christine Workman)

The export figures for the 1780s quoted above suggest a lucrative trade but fortunes were undoubtedly mixed. Timothy Cragg noted a lack of turf in the winter of 1790–91 which hit Moor Head and Lancaster in particular; 'turf they have none and coals they can get at no price'. The following year he noted the sale of goods of Richard Dickenson a 'hatter but failed of the trade' and the suicide of Joshua Rigg who worked in Thomas Procter's shop. There was a general decline in trade in the 1790s, which Cragg in 1798 blamed on the war with France and the consequent ban on imported English goods. Fortunes probably picked up thereafter before the trade really declined sometime in the 1820s and 1830s. There were no hatters left in Quernmore by the time of the 1841 census. William Birkett, of Higher Moor Head, who had traded there as a hatter for over twenty years, was listed as a farmer. By 1843 he had moved to Macclesfield, a hatting centre, and his son, James, was a woolcomber in Lancaster.[33] Other hatters left Wyresdale much earlier. Sylvester Taylor had moved to Poulton as early as the 1780s and continued his trade there. When he died in 1814 his estate was valued at £3500.[34] Some of those who remained clearly hit hard times. Edward Clarckson of Quernmore was out of work in 1831 and forced to apply for poor relief. He was sent to the workhouse at Caton and ordered to break stone for the local roads. In 1835 he asked for relief 'to travel in search of work' and was granted 5s.[35] In 1825 Thomas Gornall of Tarnbrook was listed as a hat manufacturer,[36] yet in the 1851 census he was listed as a pauper, formerly hatter, aged 78.

It is possible that some of the hatters in Over Wyresdale and Quernmore acted as commission agents for hat manufacturers in London and Stockport from the 1750s as the demand for hats grew. We certainly know that Christys of London set up one such master in Wray in 1806.

Wray

Wray, ten miles east of Lancaster is located on the River Roeburn, a tributary of the Lune. In the early nineteenth century it was a thriving, expanding industrial village of stone masons, nail makers and coal miners and witnessed a surge in population from just 483 in 1801 to 808 twenty years later. It was also an important hatting centre. The art of feltmaking was probably practised from the 1730s if not earlier and there is certainly evidence that hats were made here for over 100 years, from the 1770s to the 1870s. Unlike those involved in the agricultural dual economy, Wray hatters lived in a single community and the majority relied on the hat trade for their livelihood. For the most part the hat trade was their main, if not their sole occupation.[37]

The attractions of Wray were obvious. There was an abundance of clean water from the Roeburn, which was said to give the finished felt hats a superior gloss.[38] Local resources of turf, coal and timber provided fuel for the kettles and possibly wood for the hat blocks. Wool was probably carded in the village mill. There was easy access to markets. Some hats were evidently sold from the shop or at local markets.[39] The last hat made in Wray was reputedly purchased by a tailor in neighbouring Hornby.[40] Local fairs such as those held in Bentham at Easter and in June were also popular venues for locals to buy. 'Hats used to be placed in rows on shelves in a large piece of furniture like a clothes press, and ... hat after hat was pressed on over the forehead over the rising youth until a proper fit had been secured.'[41] The Dilworths, Gillgrasses, Parkers and Wilsons were freemen of Lancaster and could therefore trade there and through the port. Ripleys were said to have a considerable export trade, selling hats 'for the slave trade in South America' in the 1840s, though so far no records have come to light.[42] As we shall see, Wray hatters also worked for Christys and possibly other London firms on a commission basis. These firms had travellers who took and placed orders with hatters and retail outlets throughout England. There was also a good local transport network . Goods could be transported by coastal shipping from Lancaster or Glasson, by mail coach, by local carriers and by the Lancaster to Preston Canal which opened in 1797. The Lancaster to Richmond Turnpike, constructed in 1750, was close by and gave good access to the markets of the North West and over the Pennines into Yorkshire. Hats were packed in special boxes on carts, smaller hats being packed inside larger ones.

Masters and workshops

From the 1740s there were clearly close connections between Wray and members of hatting families of Over Wyresdale and Quernmore. Many were probably young, mobile single men. One such, for example, was Timothy Birkett. Born in Over Wyresdale in 1751 of Quaker stock, he was a grandson of William Birkett of Higher Moor Head (his two older brothers continuing the hat trade there). He married in Wray in 1774, carried on the hat trade at Wray until at least 1776, but had returned to Quernmore by 1779, for reasons which remain unclear, where he remained until 1802. By 1807 he and his son, Thomas, had moved to Manchester to continue their trade there.[43]

By 1800, several families had emerged who were to form the backbone of the hatting community. The Quaker influence on the trade continued to be clearly seen in the presence of the Wilcocksons, Dilworths, and Knowles families. Like Timothy Birkett, the latter two had family connections with hatters in Over Wyresdale. James Dilworth (1717–1789), a feltmaker, was a younger son of Thomas Dilworth (1660–1726) who farmed at Moor Head in Over Wyresdale. He was resident there at the same time as William Birkett, so it is possible that he was involved in the hat trade or at least that his son James learned his trade there. We do not know when James moved to Wray, though his first child, Thomas, also a hatter, was born in Wray in 1740.[44] Not all incomers were Quakers, however. John Lucas, for example, who was to establish the longest standing workshop in the village, married Elizabeth Willson in Wray in 1774. Henry Briscoe was another incomer. As the trade increased sons of local families also took up the trade. Robert Ripley, whose hat business was the last to close in Wray, was the son of a stonemason; Anthony Furness was the son of a clogger. John Wilson, whose family was involved in the trade until at least the 1830s and who was made a freeman of Lancaster in 1789–90, came from husbandman stock. As well as these families 12 other hatters are mentioned in the parish registers before 1800.

The first decade of the nineteenth century witnessed the arrival of yet more families. The most significant was that of John Mason, a Quaker who had family connections with Quernmore. His position was uniquely important in that he managed a new workshop in Wray for the London hat manufacturing firm of Christy from 1806 and the establishment of this may well have been the major impetus for the migration of the other hatting families to Wray at this time and for the taking up of the trade by locals.

Christy & Co. had been established in 1773 by Miller Christy, in Bermondsey.[45] Like other London hat manufacturers, Christy had used commission agents to make the felt bodies and since 1797 had employed the Stockport firm of Thomas Worsley. Christy sent him raw materials, ready weighed for the type of hat required. Worsley then employed local hat masters to make up the wool bodies for the Beaver hats and shipped the hats back to Christy for finishing. As demand for hats increased in the early nineteenth century Christy opened more country workshops to supplement their production, first in Frampton Cotterell, conveniently located near the port of Bristol, and subsequently in Wray.

Why did Christy choose this small rural village? It was, after all, a considerable distance from Chester where the first provincial hatters set up their trade in the sixteenth century and the Stockport/Manchester area where, apart from London, hatting had developed most rapidly in the eighteenth century. Possibly it was the existence of outworkers here, but more likely the answer lies in the Quakers' close-knit community which brought together members from all of the country and in the links which this helped to forge between London and provinces. Both Mason and Christy were devout Quakers. In 1801 Mason was living in Wyresdale, but in 1802 he and his wife, Hannah, moved to London and were recommended to the Southwark Quaker Meeting, in the heart of the hat-making industry.[46] Like other hatters, they probably went to gain experience of the London trade, especially the high standard of finishing work, as well as to make business contacts with the many London firms. They were not the only local hatters to make this journey. Joseph Blacow, although not a Quaker, was made a freeman of Lancaster in 1789–90 whilst he was living in Southwark and by 1795 had established himself in his home town as a master hatter. Thomas Mason, John's brother, had already preceded him earlier in 1802.[47] Significantly the Southwark Meeting met in Gracechurch Street which also contained Thomas Christy's factory at no. 35. It is inconceivable, therefore, that the Masons and Christy did not meet. Indeed, Christy might even have employed Mason.

In 1804 Mason returned to the district, but settled not in his home district of Quernmore but in Wray, with which he also had strong family connections. His wife, Hannah, the daughter of Robert Knowles, a hatter, was a native of Wray. John's brother, Thomas, having returned from London in 1804, and his brother in law, Robert Knowles, were already in Wray.[48] One can only conjecture that these men formed the nucleus of the Christy workshop, which John Mason ran until 1822. Christy & Co. pulled out of Wray in 1822 and Mason moved to Bradford. It is not known who took over the workshop, although it may have been one of Mason's employees by the name of Parker. If so, this was probably Henry Parker, listed in 1828 as a hatter.

As well as Christy's premises there were probably between four and six workshops in operation at any one time between 1800 and 1840. It is difficult to date their ownership with any certainty since hatters, such as Robert Ripley, are known to have worked for other master hatters in the village before branching out into their own workshops. Likewise a shop may have kept its colloquial name, even though other hatters may have rented it. Baines's Lancashire directory of 1825 lists four hat manufacturers: Henry Briscoe, Thomas Dilworth, Robert Ripley, Jr. and Christopher Wilson.[49] The first three are named again in Pigot's Directory of 1828, though Henry Parker had replaced Christopher Wilson.[50] Neither of these lists can be complete, however, since we know that the Lucas family owned a workshop which lasted nearly 100 years. These five shops together with those of Robert Knowles and Wayman (or Wainman) are also referred to in two articles in the *Lancaster Guardian* in the late nineteenth century. Most hatters rented their workshops; only John Lucas is known to have owned his. The association of name with a workshop indicated status and it is likely that the hatter was a master craftsman.

As in Quernmore and Over Wyresdale, a close-knit community is revealed in the pattern of renting and ownership. Several generations of the Knowles family were hatters or felt makers, Robert being a family name. William Wainman (1775–1821) married John Lucas's daughter, Jenny. There is some suggestion that Henry Parker, or his son, Robert, was a partner with Wainman in 1837. Briscoe's could initially have been named after Samuel Briscoe who was known to be in Wray in 1780, or his son Henry, who went bankrupt in 1831. He and Robert Knowles rented a house, barn and other buildings in Wray from Robert Furness, a clogger, in 1818, but it is not clear if this was where they had a workshop.[51] That property was inherited in 1819 by Anthony Furness, a hatter, who remained in the trade in Wray until his death sometime after 1851.

Robert Ripley (1794–1845), who inherited three houses and outbuildings in 1831, probably started Ripley's business. Two of the houses were occupied in 1826 by hatters, one of whom, Henry Parker, was married to Ripley's sister, Betty. Could they have been working for Ripley in 1826 or were they simply renting property? By 1828 Ripley and Parker are listed as separate hat manufacturers.[52] Robert Ripley, unlike John Lucas, had several financial concerns. As well as the hat trade and public house, he continued his father's stone mason trade at the local Backsbottom Quarry. After his death in 1845 the hat business was carried on by Jane, his widow, and their son, Robert. Little is known about this period, though there was a manager there in 1845, suggesting a substantial business, and Henry Parker, the hatter and property owner, was involved in the administration of the business, as well as a brother, resident in Whitby, north Yorkshire. Could they have been sleeping partners? In 1845 they signed an agreement about Ripley's hat trade, but its content is unknown.[53]

Lucas's was carried on by first by John and then his son and grandson in turn. It had a reputation for good quality hats. At the time of his death in 1820 John Lucas owned three houses and a hat workshop. He also had £250 out at interest to support his second wife during her lifetime and left bequests of £220, with the total inventory under £600, indicating a successful business.[54] The close-knit hatting community is evident in the fact that three of his daughters married hatters in the village, although it is not known if these relations worked for the firm, which ceased trading in 1862.

The approximate positions and histories of some of these workshops can be pieced together from the two articles published in the *Lancaster Guardian* in the late nineteenth century and from information in the census schedules and Tithe Map of 1849.[55] The majority were at the end of the main street, a short distance from the River Roeburn. Christys was said to have been located here at the east end of the village, as Mason planned the 'wall adjoining the water to be 3 ft. thick till raised 6ft. high'. A well was sunk for water supply, and it is likely that other hatshops in the village used a similar source.[56] Lucas's and Ripley's workshops were located on the north side of the street, a short distance from the Roeburn bridge, Dilworth's was also on the west side of Roeburndale bridge. Ripley's was probably near the Crown and Thistle, a public house managed by the family.[57] Briscoe's was also on the north side of the Roeburn and not far from the village smithy. Robert Knowles' shop was closer to the centre of the village on the north side while Wainman's was at the west end of the village near the New Inn.

There are few descriptions of the workshops themselves. Ripley's, the last hat manufactory in Wray to close sometime in the 1870s, was reported to be a large concern with at least four kettles with the planking room on the ground floor, bowing rooms on the next floor and a packing department on the top storey. It was reported to be still standing in 1889, though it was unoccupied, and had been partly used for jobbing or hat repairing until a few years before.

Christy's records, however, provide a very full picture of their premises in Wray.[58] The firm paid for the erection of a bowing and planking shop, converted from a cottage which had previously been occupied in 1805 by Foxcroft (possibly Christopher Foxcroft, a hatter), and adjoining barn. The cottage was gutted by removing the gable end and the back kitchen to make the bow shop. Spare building material was then used to make the plank shop and wall up the barn doors. The bow shop had ten windows, eight were 2 ft. 6 inches by 18 inches and two were 18 inches by 15 inches. There was a good wooden floor eight feet above the ground, but access was by a step ladder, not a staircase. All the walls were well plastered with one coat of sufficiently haired plaster and the ceiling had two coats. The builder's quote was £83 16s. 8d.

The plank shop had foundations of 18 inches, side walls 20 inches thick, and end walls two feet thick with two flues in each end wall. This could indicate that Mason had up to four kettles, so he could be employing between 24 and 32 men at the busiest times. The seven foot high walls were made of hammer dressed stone and were "dash"d" inside and out. The plank shop had eight windows, front and back, intended to give the necessary light, with four being 4 ft. by 3 ft. and the other four being 3 ft. by 2 ft. There was one door, fitted with a lock. Although the threshold was made of stone, no flags were laid on the floor of bare earth of either workshop. Local materials, in the form of Backsbottom or Ingleton slate were used in the construction. The cost of this shop was quoted as £78 10s. 0d. John Mason employed William Nicholson, a local builder in Hornby, to do the work and it was completed by 1806.

Main Road, Wray: Several hat makers' premises were situated at this end of the village, close to the Roeburn. The sign above the house to the right reads 'Joseph Alderson, Tailor and Draper', an indication of the extent to which villages retained a variety of village craftsmen and retailers well into the inter-war period. It was washed away in the flood of 1967. Ironically the sender of the postcard commented that 'the rivers are very low'. (*Lancaster City Museums*)

Workers

Although the hat trade was an important component of the industrial scene in Wray, very little is known of its organisation and trade. It is not clear how many hatters moved to Wray or which workshops they were employed in. Henry Gillgrass, for example, hailed from Quernmore, where he was living when he was made a freeman of Lancaster in 1807–8, but he married Ann Lucas in Wray in 1809, the daughter of another local hatting master. Between 1800 and 1815, 28 other hatters can be documented as living in Wray. It is difficult to gauge how long they stayed since some were only mentioned once in sources while others appear over a span of several years. The trade was also seasonal and fluctuated with demand so numbers probably fluctuated wildly. But the actual numbers were probably considerable. Both Christy and Ripley had four kettles each and there were at least four other workshops with a minimum of one kettle each, so there was the potential to employ 96 men at the busiest times. Mechanisation came very late to the trade so that the number of hats made by one hatter did not increase substantially over time. In 1824 it was reckoned that a hatter could make eight hats a day, although some did only six and some as many as ten, depending on the style and weight of the hat and the number of hours they were prepared to work.[59] With six workshops in Wray and a minimum of one kettle each, this could result in between 50 and 400 hats produced per day, depending on the number of men employed. If, as seems likely, Christy and Ripley employed more, then local hat production could have peaked at as many 770 hats per day.

Apprentice Laws had been relaxed since 1776 to allow master craftsmen to take as many apprentices as time-served journeymen, but there is no evidence that this happened in the Lune Valley.[60] Indeed, there are very few records of apprenticeships, although John Lucas senior took Thomas Harling as an apprentice in 1797[61] and John Lucas junior had two apprentices in 1841 and 1851, one of whom was his son. In 1824 it seemed to be common practice that a master 'that has no journeymen, can keep apprentices provided he has served his time with the trade; and it is by little masters in the country that the trade is supplied and there are numbers of such in almost every town throughout England'.[62] The Quakers had their own system of apprenticeship. Thomas Dilworth offered the Lancaster Monthly Meeting take an apprentice feltmaker in 1772. Robert Knowles apprenticed his own son, Henry, in 1780, the Quakers paying the £6 fee.[63]

At the trade's peak, skilled workers in hatting were reputed to earn £3 per week. A hatter in London reported in 1824 that he earned between £2 and £3 a week as a finisher, but this fluctuated according to the season and could be as low as 32s. Those who made bodies or were ruffers earned less. His wife saved him money by 'picking the coarse hairs out that are in the stuff', otherwise he would have paid 6s. for ovals or 9s. 4d. per week for flat (crowned hats) to the picker. A fair average in the trade would not exceed £2 per week for a journeyman plus what he paid his wife or picker (i.e. £2 10s.) per week.[64] Pay in Wray was reputed to be in line with this although the demarcation between body maker and finisher was not common in Wray. Only one hat finisher and one hat trimmer, his wife, appear in the census returns. In 1851 they lived in a house owned by the Ripleys and may well have been employed by that firm. However, Lancashire women were said to have assisted in the work of lining and binding hats so it may be that the wives of hatters in Wray did this, as several were daughters of hatters. No hard evidence has come to light about this, although married women invariably gave their occupation as hatter's wife, a description which could mask such tasks as carding wool and finishing hats.

The demand for hats fluctuated throughout the year and, although we lack precise local details, it is likely that the working pattern in Wray was the same as that in the rest of the country. Hatters were in demand in spring and summer, but could be unemployed or on reduced hours for up to four months per year. There were no set hours of work. In the summer a hatter could start at 'four o'clock, and work till nine at night; others work less time' as they were paid piece rates, i.e. so much per dozen hats made, rather than by the day.[65]

Hatters had a reputation for drunkenness. The hatters' work in the plank shop was certainly thirsty work. In 1824 one John Lang suggested to a government enquiry that hatters had become more sober than their earlier brethren.'I have seen, at the time I was apprentice, when beer was brought in buckets and cans into the shop for drinking, and now there is only just what a man requires at his labour generally.'[66] In Wray

the custom was that first thing in the morning on their arrival at their several shops to cast lots who should be the drink fetcher for the day. The drink was not fetched in small jugs and bottles but in tolerably large sized milking-cans. In warm sunny weather the north side of the Roeburn was a favourite resort for drinking bouts. As far as drinking was concerned Sunday and weekday was alike. On the Sunday when the weather was favourable it was usual to carry drink into neighbouring fields where the men could sip their favourite beverage at their leisure.[67]

The beer probably came from the New Inn and the George and Dragon at the north end of Wray, and from the Crown and Thistle toward the east end, a public house the Ripley family ran from the early 1820s. In 1834 there were also five beer retailers in Wray.[68]

Nationally hatters were organised into two well-established unions by the beginning of the nineteenth century. The Fair Trade Union catered mainly for the London end of the trade while the Blue Blank Union had its strength in the Manchester/Stockport area.[69] Whether either was represented in Wray is not clear; there is only one tantalising reference to the possible presence of a union shop.[70] It may well have been Ripley's or

Lucas's. In line with many other trades where employment was seasonal and irregular hatters had a system of 'tramping'.[71] This allowed a union man to go in search of work, knowing that he would be supported *en route*. He was given a ticket or blank which entitled him to relief in towns where there were hatters in trade. Rates varied throughout the country, the highest being in London where a hatter received 5s., a bed for three nights and two pots of beer. In the country he might receive only 3d. or 6d., a beer, bread and cheese and two nights' lodging. There was a club in 'almost every town in England' where, on arrival, the hatter would go to the 'turnhouse', often a public house, where a local hatter would try to find work on his behalf. The tramping hatter would demonstrate his skills and, if successful, he paid his 'footing' of 16d. to the shop constable to buy four gallons of 4d. beer for all in the shop. It is quite possible such a system operated in Wray. Although no firm evidence has been found the village had a friendly society, the Union Society, formed in 1787 and which had 114 members by 1818. Two hatters were trustees in 1810. The society's annual walk set out from Ripley's public house in Wray in the 1830s and 1840s suggesting a connection with the trade.[72]

Decline of the hat trade in Wray

Wray's heyday was relatively short. After 1815 only one new hatting name is mentioned in the parish registers, suggesting that the golden age of the industry had passed.[73] The population of the township of Wray with Botton

Bright Morning, Wray: Another perspective on this end of the village, taken before the First World War. By this date few of the village industries remained and the population had dropped by around 50% since the mid-nineteenth century. (*Lancaster City Museums*)

fell by over 200 between 1821 and 1831 to just 586. This coincided with continued decline in Lancaster's maritime trade, and with endemic agricultural and economic depression following the Napoleonic wars. It might also have reflected the growing attraction of industrial towns such as Preston and Manchester with their perceived opportunities for work and trade. Severe winters may also have disrupted supplies.[74] Although seven families continued to ply their trade for at least another generation the trade never recovered its buoyancy. Numbers recorded in the census fell steadily and the last firm ceased trading in the 1870s.

The decision by Christy to pull out of Wray in 1822 was the major symptom, and cause, of this decline. Mason's letters to Thomas Christy in 1822 revealed his desperate situation. 'I have been a long time here with but little work', he complained, and he was reduced to begging that 'if you would please to send me an odd 6 doz. of any kind it would at this time be a help to what I have …'. A month later he wrote to say that he would have to leave Wray 'as I have nearly stopt as long as I can to leave it with credit which I am desirous to do'. Christy failed to sell the house and workshop to two prospective purchasers. One, Mr John Patchett, wanted Mason to stay and rent the premises from him, but Mason refused. It depended on Mason getting work 'which he had given up on'. He held a sale a few days later and may well have sold the setting blocks, fan blocks and 30lb. of cotton, which belonged to Christy.[75] The possibility of Christy renting out the property was also considered. Thomas Albright, a Quaker, was looking to rent just John Mason's house but cheaply, 'there being so many empty ones in Wray'. Albright also hoped that Christy would let the workshop to 'one of John Mason's late men named Parker at a low rent' as 'there is an offer made to send hatts from Edinburgh'. It is interesting to note the Quaker network in full force here. Both Albright, a sailcloth-maker, and Patchett were Quakers. It is not known who eventually bought the workshop, it may well have been Parker. In 1826 Christy bought the Stockport firm of Thomas Worsley in the heart of the hat trade. This had larger premises and better marketing networks. As far as is known, contact with Wray ceased.

There was a dramatic decline in the domestic demand for felt hats in the 1830s. Exports also fell from 53,594 in 1830 to just 11,870 in 1839.[76] Felt hats had been prized for their durability and weather proofness, but with the advent of increased coach and rail travel the man in the street could indulge in a less durable, but eminently more fashionable hat. By the 1840s a change of fashion to the silk topper had greatly affected the feltmakers' fortunes. Silk had been 'plated' on to felt since 1800, but this made the hat very heavy and cumbersome. In the 1830s, however, the new silk topper became fashionable. This was constructed of silk plush on a gossamer or cotton body and it did not require the hatters' specialist skills to make it.[77] The silk hat could be made by non-apprenticed felt hatters and at a quarter of the cost of a felt one. Even the large London and Manchester hat manufacturers were seriously affected. In Stockport Christy put its felt hatters on a four or five day week in 1846 and a hatter complained that his wages had been reduced to 15s. a week and that he had been forced to learn the silk hat trade. Until then Christy had failed to persuade its workers to learn the skills required to make silk hats.[78] In Denton and district between 1847–49 over a hundred families lost their livelihood. Wray must have been affected by these changes. Although it is possible that both types of silk hats were made in Wray it must be remembered that the local mill only spun waste silk; it did not produce silk plush. John Mason may have had the skill to make the plated silk hat, but any production was more likely to have occurred in the 1840s in response to changing consumer demands. Dilworth's shop is reputed to have made silk hats at one time.

The felt hat trade was saved in the 1850s by the introduction of the bowler hat, pioneered by Locke's of St James. This hat filled a niche in the market for a less formal hat for town wear. But the Wray hatters struggled to survive. Henry Briscoe had gone bankrupt as early as 1831.[79] He remained in the village and worked as a servant and later an agricultural labourer. Several hatting names disappeared from the village at this time. Some, like Thomas Dilworth, moved their families to Preston, where they set up their own hat business. Others, like Christopher Hartley-Smith, migrated to Manchester.[80] Of those who remained in Wray, some appeared to give up hatting, although whether this represented the older generation harvesting the fruits of past successes or necessity caused by declining trade is less clear. Henry Parker in 1841 was listed as a farmer and he also owned property in the village, but his son was still a hatter in Wray and the family then had connections with Ripleys. Likewise, Henry Gillgrass became a property owner and farmer, but his two sons continued as hatters. Richard Atkinson had a herd of cattle and money out at interest when he died in 1849.[81]

By 1851 only five of the major hatting families remained in trade in Wray and only John Lucas and Robert Ripley were employers. Only 11 hatters, two apprentices, one hat finisher and one hat trimmer were listed in the census of that year. Four of them were over 60 years old. Four worked for Robert Ripley, and the presence of the hat trimmer and hat finisher, plus a hatter lodging with them in premises owned by the Ripley family, and the employment of another two men suggests that the firm had found a new market. John Lucas employed two apprentices in 1841 and 1851. One was his son, and the other was from a local hatting family, the Towers. However, William Lucas subsequently moved to Preston and only returned when his father was ill and needed help. He was a grocer as well as a hatter and had left the village again by 1871.

Numbers continued to dwindle. By 1861 there were only six hatters in addition to Robert Ripley and John Lucas. The majority were aged over 50. Ten years later, Robert Ripley and three hatters, all over 60, were left to carry on a trade which had finally been mechanised nationally. Although many parts of the hat-making process were still done by hand, it had now became a factory-based industry which small rural workshops could not compete with. The decline in trade coincided with the ageing of the hat-making population of Wray and a reluctance on the part of their offspring to follow in their footsteps, most children preferring to move away or work in the silk mill.[82]

Conclusion

There are virtually no physical remains of the district's once thriving hat industry. It has also largely disappeared from the inherited oral tradition. Yet, as we have seen, hat-making was once an important occupation which, at its peak, employed several hundred people, supported the agricultural economy, was responsible for the rapid growth of Wray, and probably enriched several of its masters. The hatters of the Lune Valley, Quernmore and Over Wyresdale were also not the only hatters in this region. Others were certainly present at Middleton to the west of Lancaster, in the Bentham area and around Masongill, and, slightly further afield in the region, in the Fylde, at Ulverston and Preston. Ongoing research is intended to produce a fuller assessment of the industry's geographical extent, and importance in the industrialisation process and the expansion of overseas markets in the late eighteenth and early nineteenth centuries. Felt hat-making was typical of much industrial production during this period in that it was geographically dispersed and relied primarily on the exploitation of hand technology rather than the water or steam-powered mechanisation. When the latter did occur after the mid-nineteenth century, it also did so against the background of changing fashions which together sealed the fate of rural workshops described here. But the fact that they disappeared does not diminish the significance of their earlier presence.

Notes

1. J. H. Smith, 'The Development of the English Felt and Silk Hat Trades 1300–1912', Unpublished PhD Thesis, Manchester University, 1980, p. 9.
2. P. M. Giles, 'The Felt-Hatting Industry c. 1500–1850 with particular reference to Lancashire and Cheshire', *TLCAS*, Vol. 69, 1959.
3. D. Corner, '"The Tyranny of Fashion": The Case of the Felt-Hatting Trade in the Late Seventeenth and Eighteenth Centuries', *Textile History*, Vol. 22(2), 1991, pp. 155–164.
4. Select Committee on Artisans and Machinery, Second Report; PP 1824 v, p. 96. Evidence of John Lang.
5. N. Penney (ed.), *The Household Account Book of Sarah Fell of Swarthmoor Hall* (Cambridge University Press, 1920), pp. 88, 166.
6. Several contemporary accounts have been used to reconstruct the process which is presented here in a much simplified form: 'The Manufacture of a Beaver Hat', *The Saturday Magazine*, 10 January 1835; *The Book of Trades or Library of Useful Trades*, Vol. 1, 1811 (Wiltshire Family History Society); Andrew

Ure, *Dictionary of Arts, Manufactures and Mines* (London, 4th edition, 1853), pp. 993–5. I would like to thank George Niven for invaluable comments on an earlier draft of this section.

7. J. Vero, *A Concern in Trade: Hatting and the Bracebridges of Atherstone, 1612–1872* (Warwickshire Books, 1995).

8. LRO, QAM/1/29/1. Admissions Register, Lancaster County Lunatic Asylum, 1816–1823.

9. Lancaster City Reference Library, MS5546. Accounts of the Brig 'Lively' (1781–82) and the Brig 'Lark' (1779–81). Logwood originated from Central America but was grown for export in the West Indies from the early eighteenth century.

10. A description by Dorothy Richardson in 1778 described how the hat having been dried was singed, then 'rubbed over with pumice to take off the coarse nap, then rubb'd with sealskin to lay the nap still finer and lastly carded with a fine card'. In M. Ginsberg, *The Hat: Trends and Traditions* (Studio Traditions, 1990), p. 70.

11. 'Rolls of the Freemen of the Borough of Lancaster 1688–1840', *Record Society of Lancashire and Cheshire*, Part. 1, A-L, Part II, M-Z, Vols 87 & 90 (1935 & 1938).

12. Lancaster City Reference Library, Lancaster Apprenticeship rolls 1736–1754; MS 161 Lancaster Corporation Enrollment Book of Apprentices as Freemen 1812–1853.

13. M. Elder, *The Slave Trade and the Economic Development of Eighteenth Century Lancaster* (Ryburn, 1992).

14. Bodleian Library, Oxford, MS477 (Sherard), p. 56. Christopher Sherson of Lancaster supplied the 'Thomas' bound for St Kitts with negro hats.

15. PRO, CO 5/749 Pt II, E/190/1359/16; J. D. Marshall, *The Autobiography of William Stout of Lancaster, 1665–1752* (Manchester University Press, 1967), p. 282.

16. PRO, CJ 1713–1736. Great Britain Exchequer Comptrollers Book of Entries within the Town and Port of Lancaster of Merchandises Going Out and Coming In.

17. M. M. Schofield, 'The Letter Book of Benjamin Satterthwaite of Lancaster 1737–1744', *HSLC*, Vol. 113, 1961, pp. 125–67.

18. N. Dalziel, 'Trade and Transition, 1690–1815', in A. White (ed.), *A History of Lancaster 1193–1993* (Keele University Press/Ryburn, 1993), p. 101. Not all local hatters were successful. One George Deyes, a feltmaker, was gaoled for debt in 1719 (LRO, QJB/7/55).

19. Lancaster City Reference Library, MS 239. Rawlinson Voyage Book no. 3, 1785–89.

20. LRO, WRW/L 1809 Christopher Sherson. All subsequent WRW references are to wills and inventories.

21. J. Thirsk, 'Industries in the Countryside', in F. J. Fisher (ed.), *Essays in the Economic and Social History of Tudor and Stuart England* (Cambridge University Press, 1961), pp. 70–88.

22. Rev. D. Schofield, 'History of Over Wyresdale' (Reprinted from *Lancaster Guardian*, 1909).

23. LRO, WRW/A 1726 William Birkett; WRW/A 1731 Ann Birkett.

24. LRO, WRW/A 1769 Francis Gibson.

25. LRO, WRW/A 1769 Francis Gibson (will).

26. LRO, WRW/A 1767 John Greenall.

27. *Lancaster Gazette*, 15 October 1836, p. 1. Sale notice of Greenalls and Hatter's shop occupied by Joseph Kirby.

28. LRO, F. Mason, *The Story of Janet Crag and Some of her Descendents* (nd. Private Publication).

29. LRO, DDX/760/1 Cragg of Ortner Family Memobook 1698–1816.

30. LRO, WRW/A 1815 William Birkett.

31. LRO, DDX 240/41 Lancaster St Mary Marriage Register 1754–1837. 28 August 1787, John Townley, hatter, widower, married Lucy Wood, widow, both of Tarnbrook, Wyresdale. It was witnessed by Abraham Swinglehurst, a hatter, whose subsequent marriage in 1790 was witnessed by John Townley.

32. LRO, DP114. Apprentice Indenture of Thomas Gornall, 1787.

33. Lancaster City Reference Library, MS 260. List of Freemen 1823–1932.

34. LRO, WRW/A 1814 Sylvester Taylor.

35. Lancaster City Reference Library. Quernmore Vestry Minutes 1830-. 9th Vestry Meeting August 1830; also January 1835.

36. E. Baines, *History, Directory and Gazetteer of the County Palatine of Lancaster*, vol. II, 1825.

37. LRO, FRL 2B xxiii. Wray Meeting Friends' Sufferings for Tithes 1738–1792. Thomas Dilworth, a hatter, in 1786 had six hattocks of wheat and oats taken in lieu of tithes.

38. *Lancaster Guardian*, 6 April 1889.

39. George Smith's Diaries, Hornby Castle Muniments (from transcript in private hands). Smith, a resident of Wray, bought a hat from Robert Ripley on 3 April, Easter Sunday, 1824.

40. This hat is now in Lancaster City Museum.

41. *Lancaster Guardian*, 2 December 1871.

42. *Lancaster Guardian*, Jubilee edition, 1887.

43. *Record Society of Lancashire and Cheshire*, Vol. 87 (1935), Rolls of the Freeman of the Borough of Lancaster, 1688–1840. Entry for 1806–7.

44. J. D. Abbatt, *A Victorian Quaker Courtship* (William Sessions, York, 1988), family tree of the Dilworths of Thornley and Wyresdale.

45. Anon, *175 Years of the House of Christy* (n. d.).

46. LRO, FRL 2B ix/13. Receipt for Removal Certificate addressed to Lancaster Quaker Monthly Meeting for John and Hannah Mason, Southwark.

47. LRO, FRL 2B x/6. Receipt for Removal Certificate from Lancaster for Thomas Mason, Southwark, 1802.

48. LRO FRL Shelf B, Safe 1, Certificates of Removals granted by Lancaster Monthly Meeting 1780–1900.4th 6m 1804 Removal to Settle (responsible for Wray at that time) for John and Hannah Mason and their son, Thomas Mason, and Robert Knowles.

49. Baines, *Directory*, p. 664.

50. *Lancashire Directory* (Pigot & Co., 1828).

51. LRO, WRW/L 1819, Robert Furness.

52. *Pigot's Directory*, 1828.

53. George Smith's Diaries, Vol. 4, 1845–1856, 10 July 1845.

54. LRO, WRW/L 1820 John Lukas.

55. *Lancaster Guardian*, 16 March 1889.

56. Stockport Heritage Library, Christy Collection. B/P/2/28. (hereafter, Christy Collection)

57. LRO, QSB/3 Alehouse Recognizances 1828.

58. Christy Collection, B/P/2/28.

59. Christy Collection. B/P/2/28.

60. Vero, *Concern in Trade*, p. 87.

61. Lancaster City Reference Library. MS 158, Apprentice Registers 1783–1812.

62. Select Committee on Artisans, 1824, p. 87. Evidence of John Bowler, hat manufacturer.

63. LRO FRL Lancaster Monthly Meeting Minute Book 1766–1777, 7th 7m 1772; FRL Lancaster Monthly Meeting Minute Book, 1777–1787, 6th 2m 1780.

64. Select Committee on Artisans, 1824, p. 87. Evidence of John Bowler.

65. Select Committee on Artisans, 1824, p. 97. Evidence of John Lang, hat finisher.

66. Select Committee on Artisans, 1824 p. 98. Evidence of John Lang.

67. *Lancaster Guardian*, 16 March 1889.

68. *Northern Counties Directory* (Pigot & Co., 1834).

69. A. Marsh, V. Ryan & J. B. Smethurst, *Historical Directory of Trade Unions*, Vol. 4 (Scolar Press, 1994), p. 477.

70. LRO, DDQ13, *Quernmore Parish Magazine*, August 1887. Articles on the history of the hat trade refer to a commission shop and a union shop in a 'nearby village' (Wray?).

71. E. J. Hobsbawm, 'The Tramping Artisan', *Economic History Review*, Second Series, Vol. 3, 1950–51, pp. 299–320. Additional information from 1824 Select Committee.

72. LRO, QDS/1/1/124. Wray Union Society. Additional information from George Smith's Diaries.

73. LRO, m/f 2/109; m/f 9/20. Melling Parish Registers, 1677–1818. Hornby St Mary Roman Catholic Registers, 1757–1855.

74. George Smith noted in his diary entry of 8 February 1823 that the roads were blocked for two days by snow.

75. Christy Collection, Correspondence 1822.

76. Christy Collection. Petition to the House of Commons by the Hat Manufacturers of Oldham and Manchester, 1845.

77. Smith, 'Felt and Silk Hat Trades', p. 302.

78. Christy Collection. B/PP/4/3. W. Barker, *The Chronicles of Canal St from BC (Before Christy's) to 1868* (reprinted 1965), p. 19.

79. *Lancaster Gazette*, 9 July 1831.

80. LRO, m/f 2/109–110. Melling Parish Registers, 1677–1833.

81. LRO, WRW/L. 1849 Richard Atkinson.

82. In the 1861 census, William Swindlehurst, aged 52 was a hatter, but both his children worked in the silk mill.

CHAPTER SEVEN

Textile Mills

James Price

Since the publication of *The Industrial Archaeology of the Lune Valley* in 1983 a considerable amount of additional research has been carried out on the development of the local textile industry, in both Lancaster itself and the surrounding rural districts, with particular interest in the late eighteenth and early nineteenth centuries.[1] The area covered by this chapter, therefore, extends beyond the strict confines of the Lune Valley itself, to incorporate areas such as Nether Wyresdale, Bentham in North Yorkshire, and Holme and Beetham in Cumbria, a district which more accurately represents the historic sphere of influence of the county town. The aim of the first half of this chapter is to provide a revised description and analysis of the textile industry in these rural areas using, as in 1983, the three stage model of domestic, water and steam power phases described by Wilfred Smith, with special emphasis on water and steam.[2] Each of these phases had a temporal dimension as well as a distinctive spatial pattern. In additon to technology and power, however, there were other locational factors which helped to determine the nature and operation of local industry: raw materials; markets; transport; labour supply; and sources of capital. Each of these factors can be applied to textiles and their analysis helps us to understand the significant features that were important in stimulating industrial development locally. The second half of the chapter describes in more detail some of the sites associated with textile production in the district. Although the Lancashire textile industry is usually associated with cotton, what is striking about the district around Lancaster is the variety of fabrics produced, incorporating silk, cotton, linen, woollens and, by the later nineteenth century, oilcloth production.

The growth of local industry

By the late sixteenth century Lancashire already had a thriving domestic textile industry dependent on local wool to the east, and, to the west, the production of linen on the Lancashire plain and the Fylde using local flax.[3] By the early 1700s, however, woollens were increasingly driven back to the Pennine areas of east Lancashire as the import of cotton allowed the manufacture of fustians (a cloth with a linen warp and cotton weft) and cotton-linen cloth to develop in a belt from Rochdale to Colne. By the early eighteenth century Lancashire had become the leading manufacturer of fustians, something that was aided by the import of cotton through the ports of Liverpool and Lancaster and the ban in 1721 upon imported muslins. Fustians, however, were themselves succeeded from about 1770 by the manufacture of pure cottons, not just in the traditional fustian area, but all over Lancashire, including rural areas around Lancaster. The increasing size of the cotton industry meant an eight-fold increase in cotton imports between 1780 and 1800.

However, there is little evidence of early domestic fustian or other textile manufacture on a large scale in north Lancashire. Some woollens had been made in small rural communities in Wyresdale such as Tarnbrook, as well as in Wray and Quernmore, and linen is known to have been produced in the Lune Valley.[4] In Lancaster there was woollen stocking weaving, to which was added silk stockings after 1715. By 1759 it was reported that 'Mr Noble employs sometimes 200 hands in working up the waste (silk) for dressing and twisting mills into women's laces, ordinary stockings and

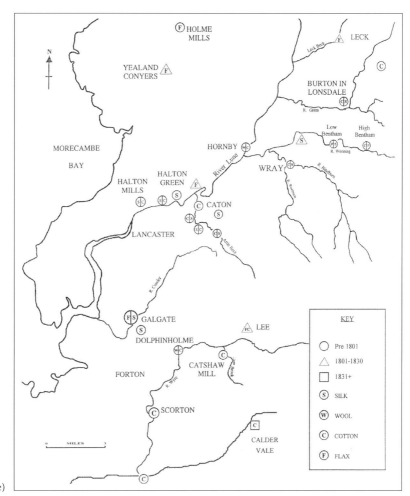

Distribution of Textile Mills in the Lancaster District (Phil Hudson from information supplied by James Price)

sewing silk'.[5] With the rise of its port, Lancaster became heavily involved in associated industries such as the manufacture of sailcloth, and workshops or factories were to be found all over the town.

Technology and power

What revolutionised rural industry in the late eighteenth century was the development of a mechanised, factory-based industry which resulted from the innovations in spinning and weaving and the application of new forms of power. Prior to this, domestic workplaces had been small, reliant on muscle power and largely situated in or around the home. The invention of the flying shuttle by John Kay in 1733, however, speeded up the process of domestic weaving and led to an increased demand for spun yarn which initiated a scramble for the invention of a spinning process to increase its output. The invention of the spinning jenny by James Hargreaves in 1763 was the first response to this but his early machines were only hand powered and could produce no more than six to eight weak threads at a time. It was the invention of the water frame in 1769 by Richard Arkwright of Preston which led to the mechanisation of the textile industry by spinning a strong yarn ideal for the warp threads Now, instead of animate power that soon tired and required rest, water power was increasingly harnessed to drive machines. Although there are early examples of mills such as Lombes mill in Derby, which worked silk with mechanical power as early as 1717, it was the construction of Arkwright's mill at Cromford in 1771 and an associated mill village and second mill in 1776 which heralded the real breakthrough. By 1787 Colquhoun's survey of textile mills identified 143 Arkwright type mills, of which 39 were in Lancashire, 23 in Derbyshire, 17 in Nottinghamshire, and 13 in Yorkshire.[6] From the end of the century, new mills ceased to rely on the Arkwright frame as much, but increasingly adopted Samuel Crompton's new spinning 'Mule', invented in 1779, which could produce yarn of a quality equal to the muslins of India. This, too, could be effectively powered by water.

Potential water power sites existed in abundance in north Lancashire, and a thriving textile industry developed from the 1780s on sites along the Lune and Wyre and their tributaries. The high rainfall, fast vigorous streams and steep, high sided valleys provided a multitude of sites although, because of the turbulent and uncertain nature of these streams, most mills were not directly on the rivers but on adjacent areas of flat land with a leet leading to them from the river. Industrial expansion in this area, therefore, was primarily associated with the water-powered phase and was consequently primarily a rural one. By 1801 the district had 22 water-powered mills to which were added a further seven by 1830. The last to be built was Calder Vale mill at Barnacre with Bonds near Garstang in 1835. In many cases existing corn mill sites were purchased for their water rights and converted into textile mills; others were on new sites. Large and small wheels were used, usually breast wheels, but there was an undershot wheel at Halton. The early mills conformed to the pattern established by Arkwright, being small and narrow (25–30 feet by 60–80 feet) and 3–4 storeys high. Built of stone with a flagged roof the wheel was either located at one end or positioned centrally with power transferred to the water frames via overhead shafts and belts.

From the early nineteenth century, however, there was an important transition to an urban-based cotton textile industry which resulted from the development of a new improved steam engine by James Watt in 1769.[7] This engine with a separate condenser used only a third of the coal used by the earlier Newcomen engine and was thus cheaper and more efficient. Within two decades it has been applied to spinning cotton with the first recorded engine installed in a cotton mill at Papplewick in Nottinghamshire in 1785. Free from the constraints of water power, mills grew rapidly in number both in existing urban areas like Manchester and in new centres like Oldham which were located on the south Lancashire coalfield. A dense canal system developed to assist in transportation. Pawson suggests that carrying coal by canal halved the cost of its transportation compared with road haulage.[8] From the 1820s, therefore, the cotton industry grew most rapidly on the coalfield situated in the central and southern parts of the county.

In north Lancashire transport improvements had a discernable impact, especially in Lancaster, but this was not sufficient to counteract the major disadvantages the district faced. Upgrading of the main roads in the district had predated the emergence of the mills. The Garstang-Heiring Syke and Lancaster-Richmond turnpikes were constructed in 1750. Improvements to the surface and alignment of a road when it was turnpiked were godsends for the transport by road of high valued products like silk from Cheshire and south Lancashire, and for the movement of cotton and flax to and from the port. The Waggon Road at Dolphinholme is a reminder of the route taken by the raw wool from East Anglia and the spun yarn to Bradford. Water transport was also used, although the rivers were not particularly suited to this. However, cotton was initially taken up the River Lune to Halton in flat-bottomed boats. The opening of the Lancaster Canal in 1797 did not stimulate large-scale economic growth in the port's hinterland but was of use to those mills along its route. In 1824, 20,000 tons of coal were brought into Lancaster by the canal.[9] The town had lacked water-powered mills, except for the Check Mill which had been sited on the headrace for the former town corn mill (in Fleet Square), but the canal coal led to a line of steam-powered mills along its route through town, since it provided easier access to coal supplies from Wigan, and increasingly coastal coal shipped via the canal spur from Glasson to Galgate. The first mill was built by Thomas Mason in 1802, to be followed later by William Jackson's Albion mill (c. 1821), Moor Lane mills (1819–31), Bath mill (1837), Queen Street mill (1840) and finally, Greenfield mill (1864). At Galgate coal was also off-loaded at the basin for both the Galgate and Dolphinholme mills.

In all about a dozen rural mills were eventually to have steam engines, but progress was slow. By 1800 only Caton Low Mill had an engine. Even by 1830 there were only four engines installed in local mills. The railways, which penetrated the area in the late 1830s and 1840s, did not lead to a marked change in fortunes, but they undoubtedly further eased access to coal and raw materials to some mills, enabling many more mills to install steam engines to augment and then replace the water wheel, so overcoming problems consequent upon drought or the freezing up of the rivers. Galgate was well placed to benefit from the opening of the Lancaster and Preston Junction Railway in 1840, as was Holme once the line was open to Carlisle in 1846, but the railway's effects on Dolphinholme and Catshaw are more difficult to discern. The Little North Western Railway Company's line from Skipton to Morecambe, opened in 1848–1850, passed directly down the Lune Valley, making it relatively easy for mills at Halton, Caton and High and Low Bentham to introduce steam power. Some of the mills which installed steam engines added an engine house and boiler house, and this prompted further extensions of other buildings to make use of the extra power and to allow the installation of new improved machinery such as throstles,[10] mules and, after about 1825, mechanised looms.

Notwithstanding the emergence of improved modes of transport and access to coal, however, the main centre of gravity of the cotton industry inexorably moved to south Lancashire. The reasons for this is are various. The area suffered from the inadequacies and subsequent decline of the port of Lancaster after the Napoleonic War, but even more importantly it lacked a good supply of local coal and the cost of transporting it from outside added to costs. As Phil Hudson explains elsewhere in this volume, much effort was expended in geological surveys in the 1820s and 1830s but none of any quantity and quality was found. The area's main period of expansion, therefore, was up to about 1830 when small rural mills were better able to survive and compete with the larger more technically advanced mills of south Lancashire because of their reliance on cheap power and labour. Thus in 1834, when the county had 650 cotton mills, there were 17 mills producing cotton in the Lancaster area. By 1862 the number in Lancashire had grown to 1979, but there were only 16 mills operating in the district. Although James Williamson and Storey Brothers continued to expand in Lancaster, there were no significant additions to the stock of rural mills. Although many survived well into the twentieth century by adopting new forms of power and diversifying into other products, the days of expansion were long over.

Materials and markets

Expansion in this district was never solely based on cotton, however. Indeed, what is striking is the variety of production incorporating silk, wool, linen, cotton and later oilcloth. Some mills continued to specialise in the same product over a long period. Flax production continued at Holme, silk (and rayon) at Galgate and Bentham until the second half of the twentieth century. Other mills, however, changed their product fairly frequently, an indication of fluctuating fortunes, the marginal nature of production locally, and changes in ownership. Thomas Higgin's mill on Moor Lane, Lancaster had switched from wool to cotton by 1828, while wool production at Dolphinholme ceased in 1853 and the mill produced cotton for its last 14 years. Willow Mill at Caton was at different times used for silk and flax before ending up as a cotton mill. Later in the century the only cotton production to survive was woven as backing for the oilcloth production carried on by Williamson's and Storeys' mills in Lancaster, and Helme's at Halton.

The raw materials for these industries were obtained from a variety of sources, although the precise origins of many of them remain unclear. Silk processing initially developed as an urban industry and was first manufactured in Lancaster around 1715 by William Noble who set up the first waste silk concern in the town.[11] He was followed by his son James, while his grandson (also a James) was, with two partners, to set up the world's first mechanised waste silk-spinning mill at Galgate. The haberdashery and hosiery made from waste silk was most probably obtained from the silk throwsters of London. Arthur Young suggested that the Kendal waste silk industry was organised by the London silk masters around 1720 in order to gain access to local cheap labour and clear water. The making up of the finished product was then completed in the capital with their own workforces. So it is highly likely that Noble initially obtained his raw material from London, but he probably became independent of the London silk makers and obtained a successful livelihood from those wealthy families involved in the developing port of Lancaster. Silk is also known to have been sold in Manchester. In addition to Galgate, by the end of the eighteenth century silk mills existed at Caton, Wray, Halton and Burton, and there was a later short-lived mill at Wennington. At Low Bentham an existing mill was later adapted from flax to silk production.[12]

We have little hard information on the sources of the raw materials for the woollen mills. It is unlikely to have been local wool, given the poor general quality of such fleeces. It may be that there is as yet an unproven link with the woollen industry of Kendal which provided raw wool or spun yarn.[13] According to Hall, the worsted mill at Dolphinholme relied on wool brought from East Anglia by cart.[14] However, in the steam-powered phase we have no information as to where Higgin's mill on Moor Lane in Lancaster, which produced high quality dress materials like Bombazine, obtained its thread. Markets are also difficult to gauge. It is likely that some of the output went overseas. In 1807 Clark noted the export of woollens and linens to the West Indies, but others were sold domestically.[15] Spun yarn from Dolphinhome was sent to Bradford in the West Riding for weaving and processing.

Flax had been grown in north Lancashire and south Westmorland since medieval times and Clark has discovered a flourishing domestic industry in the sixteenth and seventeenth centuries in and around the Lune Valley, especially at Yealand, Priest Hutton and Leck.[16] The industry was stimulated by the import of Baltic flax through the Port of Lancaster after 1750 and this eventually led to a factory-based industry with the mills at Leck, Lee, Ingleton, Burton, Galgate (Low Mill) and pre-eminently at Holme and Bentham. The output from such mills was probably largely used for sailcloth in Lancaster where there were a number of 'factories' or workshops and a handloom weaving industry, neither of which has left remains. Bailey's *Commercial Directory* of 1781 lists six makers of sailcloth in Lancaster and in 1825 Baines's *Lancashire Directory* observed that, at its peak in the 1790s, the industry produced 25,000 pieces of sailcloth each year. The industry declined dramatically, however, with the demise of the port and local shipbuilding. Baines estimated that no more than 20 pieces were produced each week by the 1820s.[17]

Raw cotton used in Lancashire originally came from the Levant and Eastern Mediterranean (Turkey and Cyprus) and later the West Indies and Brazil. In 1807 Catshaw Mill was offering for sale cotton from Surinam, Barbados and Demerara.[18] Lancaster's growing port was well placed to handle both this and the arrival of Carolina cotton from the 1740s. As well as importing directly, cotton was also transhipped from Liverpool up

Ford Ayrton & Co. Ltd, Low Bentham: Published as a postcard, this aerial view vividly illustrates the extent to which the company sought to enhance the local environment. Note the formal rose gardens by the river (bottom left), the mill workers' allotments (top centre), and the planted embankment along the road (far right). (*Lancaster City Museums*)

the Lune to St George's Quay and later via the canal from Glasson. From the 1780s the Lancaster area saw the erection of a number of cotton mills, many of them small and all using the ubiquitous water frame for spinning. In the surrounding district Caton and Halton were two important centres, as later was Calder Vale. The new larger and wider urban mills with their 'forests of columns' could more easily accommodate the mule, since the earlier Arkwright mills with at best one central row of columns had only room for two banks of frames separated by a narrow central passage. Such mills were specialist factories usually spinning yarn for sale to handloom weavers and weaving mills. With the invention of the mechanical loom by Cartwright, and its subsequent improvements from the 1820s, some mills added weaving sheds, for example, at Moor Lane South in the 1840s. Similar integrated enterprises, combining spinning and weaving, were also established at Halton, Wray, Bentham and Calder Vale.

Labour and housing

This area had a labour problem because, with the exception of Lancaster, it only had a small and scattered population. Unlike south-east Lancashire, which already had an established textile industry, the local economy was largely based on agriculture, crafts, mining and quarrying, and there was an antipathy on the part of some local people to the close supervision, long hours and rigid time discipline involved in factory work. This meant that employers often encountered difficulties in obtaining a labour force especially when, as in the case of sites like Catshaw, Dolphinholme and Calder Vale their mills were built on isolated sites.

Three strategies were adopted by employers. Firstly, if the mill was in, or adjacent to, an existing centre of population it could rely on some local labour, accommodated either in existing properties or in additonal newly-erected housing. In Lancaster there is little evidence for the factory owners building housing for their workers or even owning any. The Gregs may have owned some in the Bulk and Monmouth Street area while William Jackson built back-to-backs on Factory Hill for his Albion mill. Most workers, however, lived initially in the overcrowded and insanitary city centre and it was not until the last quarter of the century that estates like Moorland and Primrose were built as speculative ventures to house workers in the expanding canalside mills. At Caton workers came from the village and households also took in lodgers, but additional housing was built by local factory masters.[19] William Stubbs, the manager of Willow Mill, built Wesley Row in 1838 and the Gregs at Low Mill erected Thurtle and Margaret Cottages. Greg also built Croft Cottages at Broadacre with their large gardens and communal pig sty in 1831. Other properties built by mill owners or as a speculative ventures still stand at Catterall, Bentham and Holme. In Galgate, the Armstrongs, owners of the silk mill, erected the terrace of cottages on the east side of the main road sometime in the 1850s.

A second way of obtaining labour was to use pauper apprentices. In the early phrase of industrialisation, orphans and other unwanted children in workhouses, many from Liverpool and London, were put to work in some mills. They were generally boarded in an 'apprentice house', provided with food and clothing, and had a schoolmaster for their daily instruction. The best documented case locally is of Thomas Hodgson who used this method at Low Mill Caton. In 1808, 75 out of a workforce of 150 were apprentices. There are also the remains of a second Apprentice House in Caton in Copy Lane opposite Willow Mill.

Thirdly, mill owners on remote greenfield locations at prime water-power sites were obliged to follow the example of Sir Richard Arkwright at Cromford and erect housing and other facilities for their workforces. This area has a very fine assemblage of workers' housing, some built in existing villages, but others as part of these new self-contained factory villages. Dolphinholme and Calder Vale are true factory villages where the

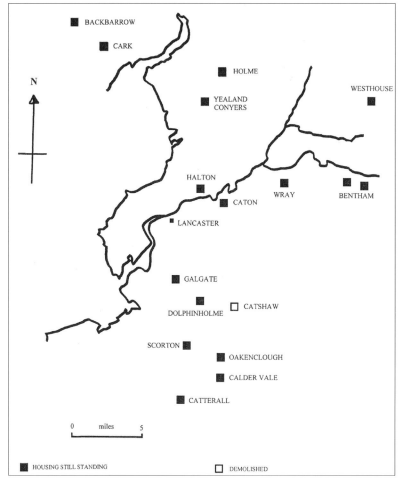

Workers' Housing in the Lancaster District (Phil Hudson from information supplied by James Price)

Lairgill, High Bentham: Originally built by the Hornby family to house workers they brought with them from Kirkham, this long terrace of two-storeyed cottages originally had cellar loom-shops where the sailcloth was woven. Joseph Carr, writing in 1893 of the early years of the nineteenth century, recalled that locals used to tease the newcomers. 'Kirkhamites, Kirkhamites, lapped up in a pen, darn't turn out to Yorkshire men.' The response was 'Yorkshirebites, Yorkshirebites, lapped up in a pen, darn't turn out to Lancashire men.' (James Price, *c.* 1983)

community from which the labour force was drawn was 'under the social and economic control of the industrialists'.[20] Dolphinholme, built around the first mechanised worsted spinning mill, is the best early example of a local mill community and was described by the factory inspector Leonard Horner in 1838 in glowing terms.

> The Mill is surrounded by the cottages of the workpeople, and they form quite a community of themselves. There is a most delicate cleanliness observed in the Mill and all about it and the whole group of homes are fresh whitewashed outside nearly every year ... the proprietors ... pay £8 a year to a clergyman, have built a chapel and a school house and maintain a schoolmaster. From all I hear it is a most virtuous and happy little colony.[21]

In addition to these pure factory villages, the scale of workers' housing at Low Bentham suggests the involvement of the mill owner. Catshaw was not a true mill village since only 15 cottages were erected for key workers while the rest of the workforce walked to work, anything up to five miles each way.[22] Workers are also known to have walked from Forton to Dolphinholme, some two to three miles each way, and there is a record

Wesley Row, Caton: Built by William Stubbs, the manager of William Thompson's Willow Mill about 1838. (*Lancaster City Museums*)

of someone walking daily from Lancaster to Crossgill, a round journey of over eight miles.

The bulk of such properties were two-storey, stone, terraced cottages with a slate roof, but at Victoria Place Halton, Gardner has identified the remains of a terrace of back-to-back cottages built as a speculative development by Joseph Robinson between 1799 and 1802.[23] The large three-storey south terrace of the Corless Cottages at Dolphinholme might have been built initially for multi-occupancy, something that may well also have been the case at Forge Mill Halton.[24]

Capital investment

Finally there is the question of capital. Where did the money for the initial investment come from? A producer had either to build or rent a mill (and it could cost as much as £4000 to build and equip a 1000 spindle Arkwright mill), purchase fuel and raw materials as well as pay his labour before getting any return. Many small enterprises elsewhere in the county were often short of capital, their production 'only earned modest profits and they were all too frequently forced out of business before being able to expand'.[25]

Locally, capital for the erection of mills came primarily from three sources. First, there were men in Lancaster who had made profits in trade or the professions who speculated in the industry. Thomas Mason, who built White Cross in 1802, and members of the Hinde family, who developed the new mill at Dolphinholme, were both merchants. Thomas Higgin, who built Moor Lane North, was the son of a long serving governor of the Castle. Gregson and Mason who financed the Ridge Lane silk mill were local solicitors. Threlfall of Bath Mill was a grocer and ironmonger, and Satterthwaite and Barrow of Queens Mill were a grocer and a wool draper respectively. Secondly, in rural areas some money obviously came from trade but other monies were invested by local landowners like the Hodgsons at Caton. In most cases these entrepreneurs had no technical skill themselves and hired managers for their expertise. Hinde at Dolphinholme employed the Derhams who, in time, became partners. Finally, families from outside the area were increasingly to be found amongst the owners. The Hornbys of Kirkham ran mills at Bentham while Ormrod of Bolton ran Scorton mill from the 1850s to 1875. There were also Preston entrepreneurs involved, including Swainson at Halton (1834–62) and Dolphinholme (1840–53) to be followed at the latter by Cooke and Margerison, and Rushton and Slater from 1853 until closure in 1867. The most significant example of outsider investment, however, was Samuel Greg who took over Low Mill Caton in 1817 and built Moor Lane South in Lancaster. He had already demonstrated considerable business acumen and established a family dynasty based on Quarry Bank Mill, Styal in Cheshire. His son John inherited the Lancaster and Caton mills and operated them until they were sold to the Storeys in the 1860s.[26]

Some major sites

The early sections of this chapter have discussed the factors which lay behind the development of the textile industries in the district. The remainder briefly describes the history and some of the buildings used by this industry in the rural area around Lancaster.[27] The Lune Valley formerly had a very complete set of remains from its industrial past including workers' housing. Since 1983 demolition and conversion have cut a wide swathe through these remains so that, for example, only three of the Lancaster canalside mills still survive. Today there are no signs of the sailcloth workshops identified by Hartley in 1970, the last of them being demolished in the early 1970s.[28] . Of handloom weaving there are no identifiable remains though some would appear to have existed in Skerton prior to its redevelopment in the 1950s and 1960s. There are a few remains of domestic industry in the rural areas, most notably in Bentham, but the attention here will be on those mills and communities which owed their origins to water power.

All the mills relied heavily on local supplies for building. Early mills had a heavy dependence on wood, with load bearing walls carrying wooden beams, joists and floors. Such mills were prey to fire given the amount of oil dripping from the machinery and the primitive methods of heating and lighting. As far as possible such mills were lit by natural light and this explains the large numbers of windows, such as are evident at Willow Mill, with candles used after dark. As well as being dangerous, such lighting was inefficient and the arrival of gas lighting was a godsend for employers as it allowed 24 hour working. Gas was installed at Dolphinholme in 1811, one of the first rural mills to have it, and it also lit the village street.[29] It was later followed by Low Mill Caton, Catshaw and Galgate. Other rural mills may also have had gas;; those in Lancaster possibly relied on the town gas works. Between 1792 and 1803 William Strutt and Charles Bage overcame much of the hazard of fire by the introduction of brick arches carrying stone/cement floors supported by cast iron beams and columns. The resultant iron-framed mills largely removed the flammable wood of earlier mills and were virtually fireproof. In addition, the use of columns and beams allowed the building of larger factories. Those at Calder Vale and Low Mill Caton are over 40 feet wide compared with the 25–30 feet of the earlier Arkwright Mills. Moor Lane Mills in Lancaster, built for Thomas Higgin in 1819 and Samuel Greg 1825–31 were both fireproofed, as was part of the earliest building at White Cross. Moor Lane North even has metal roof trusses. There is also evidence of fireproofing at Catshaw and on the ground floor at Low Mill Caton.

Dolphinholme

In 1784 a water-powered corn mill on the River Wyre at Dolphinholme was converted by Thomas Edmondson and Messrs Addison and Satterthwaite to spinning worsted yarn using Arkwright water frames. This firm was affected badly by two floods and made substantial losses. In 1795 a new firm run by Thomas Hinde, his son William, together with Messrs. Hawden and Patchett took over the lease and opened a new factory built on a site away from the river. A weir was built three-quarters of a mile upstream and a tail race led to a 30 foot water wheel, powering what was then the largest mill in the area. The remains of the gasometer tank still exist, as does the chimney. Across the road a wool-combing mill and warehouse were built with another separate warehouse across the river. The owners lived in the Woodcock Hall and both it and the manager's home, Derham House, still survive. The mill's remote location meant that owners needed to provide accommodation. Some of the workers' houses have survived on either side of the Wyre. In the 'Bottoms' there are cottages, and above the mill are the twin rows of Corless Cottages, with their attendant privies, dating from about 1796. Below the former warehouse was a number of 'cellar' dwellings created for workers and their families.

Because of problems with a fluctuating water supply a steam engine was installed in 1822. During the next decade the partnership expanded, purchasing mills in Leeds and Bradford. In 1839 a new 40 foot water wheel, 9 feet wide, was installed, but in the same year Hinde and Derham went

Calder Vale Village: Viewed from just above the road from Garstang looking over Victoria Terrace. The mill is visible through the trees to the right. The earliest cottages built during the 1830s are to the far left of the picture. (James Price, *c.* 1983)

into liquidation because of the extravagances and speculations of Robert Derham in Leeds. Dolphinholme mill was taken over by Swainsons who continued in worsted spinning to 1850. In 1853 Henry Rushton converted the mill to cotton and also built a large weaving shed. Its remote situation was against it, however. It closed in 1867 and the mill building was demolished.

Calder Vale

This is the other major local example of a mill village.[30] It remains operational today, conveying a strong impression of a mill community of over a century ago. Rows of houses stand on the valley side overlooking the mill, including the later 'Albert' and 'Victoria' terraces. The mill and its community was one of the last water-powered settlements. It was created in 1835 by the Jackson brothers, Richard and Jonathan, brothers of John who ran the local paper mill at Oakenclough. The original village included a cotton spinning mill and 'Long Row', a terrace of nineteen small stone houses. A chapel, Low Mill weaving sheds (1848, now demolished), and other cottages were added later. The four-storey Lappet Mill is of non-fireproof construction and has timber beams supported by iron columns; it is 45 feet wide and was probably built for mule spinning. A turbine, driven by the leet from the pond filled by the River Calder, later replaced the waterwheel. At the site of Low Mill is a drained mill pond and several small cottages.

Caton

The building of five mills at Caton Town End (Willow, Rumble Row, Low, Forge and Ball Lane) meant that this rapidly outgrew the existing township of Brookhouse.[31]

Willow Mill is the best local example of an early water-powered textile mill still in existence, and stands on a site which was occupied by a fulling mill in the Middle Ages. The eastern end of the present building, which is slightly higher than the rest, is probably the earliest section of the original mill, built sometime before 1790. It follows the traditional water-powered mill construction, with four storeys (including the attic), stone walls and a flagstone roof, now replaced by slates. In 1795 it was advertised for sale as a 'newly erected cotton mill' and the measurements given, 197 feet long by 25 feet wide, are approximately those of the existing L-shaped building with the millpond behind. By then there was already a mill community with 27 cottages and weaving shops, and an apprentice home for the child workers. By 1804 shops and a counting house are also recorded. Timbers about 12 inches square span the building and carry the wooden joists and floor-boards: these in turn rest on wooden posts (and later, iron columns) and on the loadbearing walls. Like all early factories Willow Mill lacked artificial light and there are thus large numbers of small paned windows (some later blocked) to let in the maximum light. The waterwheel, at the north end, was originally a breast or overshot wheel, 15 feet in diameter, which produced 20 horsepower: this was replaced after 1900 by a Gilkes Turbine. At the time of the author's major survey in 1983 the complete water system still existed, including a drained pond, now built upon, with sluices. Today, water is culverted under the mill and reappears in the yard to the north. Like Low Mill (see below), Willow Mill stands on the mill race which leaves the Artle Beck at Gresgarth Hall and then skirts the Escowbeck estate. Later an auxiliary steam engine was installed with an engine house and a chimney: the latter still stands but has been topped.

The mill was one of the largest locally, with over 10,000 square feet of working floor space. After a period of use for cotton, and later flax, it became a silk mill from 1815 to 1861, when it was turned over to bobbin-making. Work continued there until 1973, although in the last years on the production of brush heads. Other remains at this site are the former silk warehouse, and across Copy Lane the remains of the apprentice house. The mill cottages at Rock 'm Jock were rebuilt by Albert Greg in the last century, and Wesley Row, adjacent to the Methodist Chapel, was built for mill workers by the manager, William Stubbs, in 1838. The silk factor's residence, Greenfield House, still stands further down the millrace.

South-west of Willow Mill, at the end of the millrace, is Low Mill. It was originally an early Arkwright type mill measuring 81 feet by 27 feet when it was first built but what remains now was rebuilt after a disastrous fire in 1837. It is perhaps the finest of the local textile mills, although we do not know who designed it. Less vernacular in style than Willow Mill, according to Ashmore it displays many of the 'attractive features of the factory buildings of the early [factory period], symmetrically placed windows with small panes and Georgian doorways with fanlight(s) outlined in rusticated stonework'.[32] The original building was put up by Thomas

Hodgson, a Caton man who, in 1784, had purchased a farm on the side of the Lune Valley for the purpose. It was built on the edge of the flood plain of the river, while on the terrace above it, a large pond, covering 2.2 acres, provided a water supply fed by the millrace. The farmhouse itself he converted into an apprentice house to which he added dormitories.

The mill housed throstles to spin cotton, brought from Lancaster, and produced a poor quality cotton yarn. It had 2864 spindles in 1814. In 1817 it passed into the hands of the Greg family of Styal as part payment of a debt, and was run by them for spinning cotton, except for a short period in the 1840s when it was used for weaving. The Gregs modernised the mill when they took it over, building an engine house at the north end and installing a 20 horsepower Boulton and Watt engine. By 1830 they had spent £15,769. In 1837, however, fire destroyed a large part of the mill, particularly the southern end which housed much old and out-of-date machinery. The fine five-storey mill we see today is largely the result of rebuilding after this fire, which explains the two dates, 1784 and 1838, on the keystone of the door leading to the staircase turret, the latter date also appearing on the warehouse in the yard to the west of the main building. This mill is 76.5 feet long, 49 feet wide and 48 feet high, with four storeys and an attic. At roof level on the front elevation is a projection which had a removable window for a hoist, and at the south end a stone turret, added in 1838 and later topped by a sprinkler tank. The ground floor was fire-proofed, with cast iron pillars supporting jack arches which ran the length of the mill, the other storeys being of traditional construction with iron columns carrying timber beams and wooden floors. There is a timber-framed roof covered with slates.

Power was derived from the waterwheels driven by water from the large pond on the terrace and a smaller pond to the rear of the building. In the wheelpit to the south was a high water wheel (25 feet 9 inches in diameter by 7 feet 3 inches in width), and at the north end a low water wheel, possibly undershot, 17 feet 6 inches in diameter: the two wheels together produced between 18 and 55 horsepower. The tailraces from the wheels met below the warehouse, were culverted under the yard and then ran as one race along the edge of the Lune flood plain for a quarter of a mile before entering the river. The low water wheel was replaced after 1864 by a 75 horsepower Gilkes turbine, and the line of its pipe could still be seen in 1983 exiting from the wheel house, running along the rear of the mill and entering at the north end. Power was supplied to the carding and spinning machines by means of horizontal shafting, and holes in the tops of the iron columns allowed these to pass along the mill. As water power fluctuated throughout the year (and high water in the Lune could result in water backing up the tailrace), the Gregs added steam power in 1819. Later two steam engines were put a the north end, as well as a boiler house supplied with Lancashire boilers, and these necessitated the building of a large, red-brick chimney. After the purchase by Storeys in 1864, a retort

Caton Forge Mill, 1970 (cf. cover illustration): The mill after closure. The majority of the building has been restored and converted into housing. (John Crookes)

house was built to manufacture gas to illuminate the mill and part of the village. This stood to the north east of the mill, and the base of the gasometer remained as a circular pit east of the warehouse until the recent conversion. South of the mill was the manager's house, recorded on the tithe map of 1843 but rebuilt in the late nineteenth century: it stands at the edge of the millpond. As at Willow Mill the mill was sited close to the existing village to which workers' houses could be added. The houses at Broadacre, Throstle Cottages, at Margaret Fold (opposite the Ship Hotel, but now demolished) were built as a result of the existence of Low Mill. After Storeys purchased the mill it was used by them until 1970 to produce warp for weaving in Lancaster. Recently the mill complex has been sympathetically developed into a residential area of great character and attractiveness.

Forge Mill was located at the top of the mill race which terminates at Low Mill. Here, on the site of a former iron forge, a cotton mill was built around 1796 and an industrial hamlet developed. The building has been converted into three houses and is accompanied by the former manager's house, Forge House, and the nearby row of five cottages. It is a long narrow four-storey building. The oldest part contained a 16 foot wheel. After 1828 the mill was extended westwards and by 1843 had a steam engine with a chimney; at the west end is also a small bell turret. After being used for spinning cotton, silk and flax it was taken over by the Brocklebanks and used as a bobbin mill from about 1869 to 1931. Forge, Willow, Low Mill, plus the now demolished Rumble Row mill, were joined together by a mill race which comes from a weir in the Artle Beck behind Gresgarth Hall. This race still crosses into the Beck at Forge Mill on a metal launder.

Halton

The mills at Halton were once an enormous complex of buildings stretching for over half a mile down the Lune, powered by a mill race along the bank which started at Forge Weir and only re-entered the Lune at Halton Bridge.[33] They were an example of an enterprise which survived into the twentieth century by changing from one product to another. The upper part of Forse Bank Mill was spinning cotton in 1812 and two rows of cottages which were built into the valley side there probably dated from this period, as did the mill building at the top of the headrace from Forge Weir. In 1826 a sale notice mentions 12 cottages and that the mill was being used for flax and twine. This factory was powered by a wide undershot wheel. It was purchased in 1834 by Swainsons of Preston who returned it to cotton. They added a weaving shed to the north east and possibly an extension at the rear of the original mill, a building at right angles to it with small paned windows. By 1841 it employed 54 workers. From 1862, when Swainsons closed the mills, until about 1869 the factory was closed. Stockdale and Wolfendale then reopened it to make oilcloth. James Helme joined the company as a partner around 1874 and in the 1870s the firm erected two large multi-storey stone buildings further downstream facing

Halton Mills: A panorama of the riverside industrial complex at Halton when it was still in full operation. This was possibly the most developed industrial site along the Lune. Some of it remains in use as light industrial and commercial premises, but the majority has been demolished. (from a copy in *Lancaster Central Library*)

the river which were used for the manufacture of oilcloth and leather cloth. The complex continued to develop with the building of a fine brick chimney and boiler house and several single storey buildings at the south end. By 1900 there was one large complex in which the entire production of oilcloth was carried out, from the spinning and weaving of cotton at Forse Bank through to finishing at Low Mill. In 1983 most of the buildings were still standing but today only those parts of Forse Bank Mill occupied by Luneside Engineering survive.

The Low Mill at Halton, still standing by the lower weir, dates initially from 1744 but was almost completely rebuilt about 1834 by Robinson. He built the existing three-storey mill which runs parallel to the river, the buildings of which are grouped around a courtyard and include the engine house (with chimney) to the north. The original water power was provided by a leet following the river bank from Forge Bank to fill a pond at the rear of the mill (now largely filled in). The main product after 1862 until its sale in 1891 was coconut matting. It was then sold to the Helmes, who used it for offices and warehousing as well as for embossing leather cloth.

Other cotton mills

Catshaw mill was built in 1785 to exploit the Arkwright system after the patent had lapsed.[34] It was a cotton mill in a remote location on the upper Wyre. Water came from Black Clough via a three mile leet into a pond at the mill. An advertisement in the *Manchester Mercury* on 10 February 1795 gives dimensions of '63 feet in length and 29 feet in width ... three storeys (and) hath a water wheel of 18 feet two inches high and 6 feet wide ... (with) ten new spinning frames of 60 spindles each ... also 15 newly built dwelling homes'. It had a somewhat chequered career being closed between 1794 and 1797. Although it reopened, it never really evolved into a viable village community. After a further closure of nine years, a newly-rebuilt mill was erected in 1847. This was 70 feet by 29 feet, four to five storeys high. It had gas lighting and was powered by a vast wheel 150 feet in circumference (48 feet diameter) and 7 feet wide called 'Leviathan'. In 1856, however, this mill was destroyed by fire and never rebuilt. Its remote location and lack of a local labour force, with most workers walking from elsewhere, may explain its failure. Little remains except for the outline of the factory building with its 50 foot wheel pit and a drained mill pond. The remains of a line of iron columns down the centre of the mill which carried cast iron beams are also visible although, if they were an attempt to make the mill fireproof, they were clearly an expensive failure.

At Scorton, south of Lancaster, there are the remains of the cotton mill with adjacent cottages which were built about 1788. Only part of the ground floor and cellars still remain, the latter formerly the site of a water turbine. Westhouse Mill, in the upper reaches of the Lune Valley, off the A65 near Ingleton, was another example of a cotton mill erected sometime before 1800 at a location remote from a centre of textile manufacture. Originally

Wray Mill: This small mill had a chequered history spanning over a century. At the time this postcard was sent it was used for wood turning (bobbins). The sender thought it 'a very pretty view'. (*Lancaster City Museums*)

water-powered, it later had a steam engine added and ran until about 1835 when it closed. For a short time in the 1880s it made oilcloth and table baize. The building has been demolished and today only the warehouse (converted to a farm house and barn) and Post Office Row, built to house workers at the mill, survive.

Silk mills

Silk had been spun in Lancaster from the early eighteenth century but spread into the rural areas from the 1790s, with a peak of production being achieved before 1860. After this, in common with much of the English silk industry, the area was adversely affected by the signing of the Free Trade Treaty with France. Unrestrained importation of French silk led to the closure of all but the three largest factories at Bentham, Galgate and Wray.

In 1792 a corn mill on the River Conder at Galgate was purchased by three Lancaster men: John Armstrong, James Noble and William Thompson.[35] This building was rebuilt to create a two-storey mill to spin waste silk, obtained from London and Manchester, using throstles. It was the first mechanical silk spinning mill in the country. In 1832 the mill was extended eastwards with the addition of a three-storey mill of non-fireproof construction with wooden floors supported by iron columns. This was built to take the larger self-acting mules which were powered by two 10 horsepower beam engines housed in a new boiler and engine house with a square chimney built on the opposite side of Chapel Lane. In 1852 a five-storey red-brick mill with a cast iron water tank on the north-west corner was put up across the road alongside the engine house, again of non-fireproof construction. This mill, the last relic of the north Lancashire silk industry, continued spinning until 1970, albeit with nylon alongside the silk. The buildings are now used for a variety of purposes. The remains of the water power system still exist, with a race from the Conder feeding a millpond to the north; the tailrace, after passing under the corn mill, flows back into the Conder. The workers' housing was built along Chapel Street and the main turnpike (now the A6).

At Wray the remains of the silk mill were converted in 1980 into housing while the Halton silk mill is no longer recognisable as an industrial building, having long been converted into a private house. We have little evidence about Wennington's short-lived mill which operated c. 1821–23, although its site could well have been adjacent to the corn mill there. At Low Bentham the mill was originally water-powered with a leet off a weir on the River Wenning. The later fire engine house and topped chimney still stand, together with the weaving sheds and warehouses.

Flax mills

Mills for the production of linen were built where the domestic industry was strong: where it was not, the factory could fail, as at Moorside, Caton in 1807. Linen manufacture continued longest at Holme, north of Lancaster, and just over the Yorkshire border at High Bentham. At the latter flax was processed from about 1750 and by 1814 as it become an important part of business empire run owned by the Hornbys of Kirkham. It was they who built Lairgill, a terrace of 16 two-storeyed cottages with cellar loom-shops in the village where the linen was originally woven. Waithmans ran the mill from 1851–66. After 1876 spun yarns were used for belting and hosepipes, the predecessors of the firehose industry of today. On Wenning Road is a set of early cottages associated with the mill.

At Holme mills, which began working flax about 1790, the central, four-storeyed, non-fireproof mill was rebuilt after a fire in 1860. The Waithman family were involved here also. The location of this mill, adjacent to the line of the canal, provided it with good transport facilities, further improved by a tramway to Holme railway station, which can still be seen as a broad open path running parallel to the road. On the canal at Sheernest and adjacent to the mill are some fine examples of early workers' housing.

At Yealand there is an interesting survival which links together the water-powered phase and steam-powered industry. Opposite the Roman Catholic church, and facing Waithman House, stands a row of two-storey stone cottages. These unobtrusive dwellings were formerly handloom weavers' cottages, where linen cloth was produced. Adjacent to the cottages and at right angles to them is a large two-storey, barn-like building with several blocked-up windows: this is the mill built by Waithman in 1825 and powered by a steam engine, which was designed to increase the output of yarn for these and similar handloom weavers. After 'retting', to loosen the fibrous material, 'scutching', and drying, the longer fibres were then spun into linen yarn.

Bobbin making

With the decline of the rural textile industry in the nineteenth century bobbin making spread into the Lune Valley and must have helped ease rising unemployment. Bobbins were used to hold the spun yarn before it was woven into cloth. Bobbin making had come into the area from Furness by 1820 and usually made use of existing mills.

At Crossgill an existing corn mill was converted to bobbin making sometime before 1841. Although the mill has disappeared, the headrace and weir for the water supply can still be traced, and the early coppice wood shed, with its circular pillars and flagged roof, still stands. Another example was Lordship Bridge where a seventeenth-century farmhouse, possibly an earlier mill, was converted for bobbin making by adding a two-storey building at the end, at right angles to the existing house, with a breast wheel on one side to provide power. The former textile mills of Rumble Row, Willow and Leck were similarly converted, while at Cowan Bridge, the former Clergyman's Daughters' School, once attended by the Bronte sisters, made bobbins for a time. Millhouses, a mile beyond Wray on the River Hindburn, was another small settlement with a bobbin mill. All these mills used water power and coppice wood, and the men worked at wood lathes in front of windows for light.

After 1870 this trade declined in its turn, partly because of decreased demand and the importation of bobbins from Scandinavia, and partly because of the appearance of metal bobbins or cheaper bobbins made of compressed paper. Many mills closed: others diversified. Willow Mill, as we have seen above, made brush heads. A few continued, however, well into the twentieth century. Millhouses operated until the 1940s, and Royds Mill at Heysham remained open until 1970. This used steam and electric power, and the mill itself was single-storeyed with a red-brick Lancashire boiler house and chimney.

Conclusion

The textile industry which expanded from the late eighteenth century has left a tangible imprint on the local landscape. Although none of the mills is still in production, and some of them have been demolished, they helped to create new residential communities which continue to be inhabited today and which continue, therefore, to provide a direct link with the past. We now know a considerable amount about how they operated, and who owned them, but there is still scope for further research into this fascinating aspect of the district's heritage.

Notes

1. J. W. A. Price, *The Industrial Archaeology of the Lune Valley* (CNWRS, University of Lancaster, 1983). Other work on rural mills is footnoted below. For recent work on Lancaster see especially A. R. Mousdale, 'Textile Mill Architecture in Lancaster and its Hinterland: a preliminary survey', Unpublished Dissertation, Diploma in Industrial Archaeology, Institute of Industrial Archaeology, University of Birmingham, 1988 (copy in Lancaster Library); P. J. Gooderson, *Lord Linoleum: Lord Ashton, Lancaster and the Rise of the British Oilcloth and Linoleum Industry* (Keele University Press, 1996); J. W. A. Price, 'Industry and Changes in its Location in Nineteenth-Century Lancaster', *Contrebis*, Vol. XX, 1995, pp. 39–47; J. W. A. Price, *Industrial Lancaster* (Lancaster City Museums, 1989).

2. W. Smith, *An Economic Geography of Great Britain* (Methuen, 1949).

3. M. C. Higham, 'The Organisation and Production of Textiles in North-West England in the Medieval Period, including Woollen Processing, but with Particular Reference to Linen', in E. Roberts (ed.), *A History of Linen in the North West* (CNWRS, Univerasity of Lancaster, 1998), pp. 1–21.

4. M. Robinson, 'The Linen Industry in North Lancashire and Cumbria, 1660–1830', in Roberts (ed.), *Linen in the North West,* pp. 44–65

5. J. Nelson, 'The Demand for Silk and the Waste Silk Industry in Eighteenth-Century Lancaster, 1711–1780', *Lancashire Local Historian,* 1985, pp. 24–31. See also the same author's 'An Introductory Survey of the Silk Industry in Eighteenth-Century Lancaster', *Contrebis* (Lancaster Archaeological Society), Vol. 10, 1982, pp. 14–26.

6. S. D. Chapman, 'The Arkwright Mills – Colquhoun's Census of 1788 and Archaeological Evidence', *Industrial Archaeology Review,* Vol. VI (1), 1982, pp. 5–27.

7. J. W. A. Price, 'Boulton and Watt Engines in North Lancashire: an Industrial Mystery', *Contrebis,* Vol. XVII, 1992, pp. 27–37.

8. E. Pawson, 'The Framework of Industrial Change, 1730–1900', in R. A. Dodgshon and R. A. Butlin (eds), *An Historical Geography of England and Wales* (Academic Press, 1978), p. 409.

9. *Lancaster Gazette,* 20 January 1825.

10. The throstle was essentially an improved water frame which was larger, had a simpler drive system and higher spindle speeds. It largely replaced Arkwright's water frame after 1800.

11. Waste silk is the term given to that part of the silk moth cocoon that could not be easily be drawn as a continuous filament because of the natural glue secreted by the moth. To dress and throw this silk it was first necessary to boil the cocoons to break down the glue.

12. E. R. & J. H. P. Pafford, *Employer and Employed: Ford, Ayrton & Co. Ltd, Silk Spinners, with Worker Participation, Leeds and Low Bentham, 1870–1970* (Pasold Research Fund, 1974).

13. M. Davies-Shiel, *Wool is my Bread: a History of the Growth of Kendal's Woollen Trade up to 1575* (Kendal, 1975).

14. P. P. Hall, 'Dolphinholme: A History of the Dolphinholme Worsted Mill, 1784–1867', *Transactions of the Fylde Historical Society,* Vol. 112, 1960.

15. C. Clark, *An Historical and Descriptive Account of the Town of Lancaster* (1807), p. 63.

16. D. M. Clark, 'The Economic and Social Geography of Rural Lonsdale, 1801–61', Unpublished MA Thesis, University of Liverpool, 1968.

17. E. Baines, *History, Directory and Gazatteer of the County Palatine of Lancaster*, Vol. 2 (1825), p. 26.

18. Personal communication from Paddy Buckley.

19. P. J. Gooderson, 'The Social and Economic History of Caton, 1750–1914', Unpublished MA Dissertation, University of Lancaster, 1969.

20. S. Pollard, 'The Factory Village in the Industrial Revolution', *English Historical Review* (89), 1964.

21. Quoted in C. Aspin, *Lancashire: the First Industrial Society* (Helmshore Local History Society, 1969), pp. 133–4.

22. P. Buckley, 'Catshaw Factory', *Contrebis*, Vol. XVIII, 1993, pp. 62–91.

23. N. Gardner, *Halton-on-Lune: a Study of Water-Powered Industry between the thirteenth and twentieth Centuries* (Privately Printed, *c.* 1983), pp. 1–21.

24. J. W. A. Price, 'Industrial Housing in Rural Areas: a Case Study of the Lancaster Area', *Contrebis*, Vol. XII, 1986, pp. 11–22.

25. G. Timmins, *Four Centuries of the Lancashire Cotton Industry* (Lancashire County Books, Preston, 1996), p. 52.

26. For a history of the Gregs, see M. B. Rose, *The Gregs of Quarry Bank Mill* (Cambridge University Press, 1986).

27. For a full description of Lancaster's canal mills see Price, *Industrial Archaeology of the Lune Valley*, pp. 30–37.

28. Map drawn by T. Hartley *c.* 1970 and reproduced in J. W. A. Price, *Industry and Changes in its Location in Nineteenth-Century Lancaster*, p. 43.

29. A. S. Bennett, *Dolphinholme in 1811* (2nd edition, Manchester District Junior Gas Association, 1986).

30. J. M. Beeden, 'The Origins of Calder Vale and Oakenclough: the Nineteenth-Century Houses of Calder Vale and Oakenclough', *Contrebis*, Vol. VIII, 1980, pp. 63–72; 'The Origins of Calder Vale and Oakenclough: the Nineteenth Century', *The Over Wyre Historical Journal*, Vol. III, 1985, pp. 20–24; J. Wilcock, *The Story of Calder Vale and Oakenclough* (Privately published, 1997).

31. P. J. Hudson and J. W. A. Price, 'The Mills on Artle Beck, Caton', *Lancashire Archive* (7), Lightmoor Press, 1995, pp. 48–58; 'Wilmans of Willow Mill, Caton', *Archive* (12), 1996, pp. 25–46; Price, *Industrial Archaeology of the Lune Valley*, pp. 14–22.

32. O. Ashmore, *The Industrial Archaelogy of Lancashire* (David & Charles, 1969), p. 44.

33. J. W. A. Price, 'Forge Bank Mill, Halton (1)', *Contrebis*, Vol. VIII, 1980, pp. 33–40; 'Forge Bank Mill, Halton; a Correction', *Contrebis*, Vol. X, 1982, p. 49; 'Forge Bank Mill, Halton (2)', *Contrebis*, Vol. XVII, 1990, pp. 25–29.

34. Buckley, 'Catshaw Mill', *passim.*

35. J. M. Beeden, 'Galgate Silk Mills: a Study of the Development of Mill Architecture', *The Over Wyre Historical Journal* (Pilling and District Historical Society), Vol. VI, 1991, pp. 39–48; P. J. Hudson, 'A Previously Unrecorded Silk Mill in the Lower Lune Valley', *Contrebis*, Vol. XVIII, 1993, pp. 46–51.

Name and Place Index

Local Surnames

Places

(extended treatment in bold; illustrations in italics)

Occasional Papers from the Centre for North-West Regional Studies

The Centre for North-West Regional Studies, based at Lancaster University, brings together members of the university and the regional community. As well as its extensive publication programme of books and resource papers, it organises conferences, study days and seminars covering a wide range of subjects. For a small annual subscription 'Friends of the Centre' receive regular mailings of events and discounts on books and other activities.

For further details contact Centre for North-West Regional Studies, Fylde College, Lancaster University, Lancaster, LA1 4YF; tel: 01524 593770; fax: 01524 594725; email: christine.wilkinson@lancaster.ac.uk; Web site: www.lancs.ac.uk/users/cnwrs.

Hadrian's Wall: A Social and Cultural History, 2000, Alison Ewin	£8.50
Furness Abbey: Romance, Scholarship and Culture, 2000, C. Dade-Robertson	£11.50
Rural Industries of the Lune Valley, 2000, ed. Michael Winstanley	£9.95
The Romans at Ribchester, 2000, B. J. N. Edwards	£8.95
The Buildings of Georgian Lancaster, (revised edition), 2000, Andrew White	£6.95
A History of Linen in the North West, 1998, ed. Elizabeth Roberts	£6.95
History of Catholicism in the Furness Peninsula 1127–1997, 1998, Anne C. Parkinson	£6.95
Vikings in North-West England – The Artifacts, 1998, B. J. N. Edwards	£6.95
Sharpe, Paley and Austin, A Lancaster Architectural Practice 1836–1942, 1998, James Price	£6.95
Romans and Britons in North-West England, (revised edition), 1997, David Shotter	£6.95
Victorian Terraced Houses in Lancaster, 1996, Andrew White and Michael Winstanley	£6.95
Walking Roman Roads in the Fylde and the Ribble Valley, 1996, Philip Graystone	£5.95
Romans in Lunesdale, 1995, David Shotter and Andrew White	£6.50
Roman Route Across the Northern Lake District, 1994, Martin Allan	£5.95
Walking Roman Roads in East Cumbria, 1994, Philip Graystone	£5.95
St Martin's College, Lancaster, 1964–89, 1993, Peter S. Gedge and Lois M. R. Louden	£5.95
Lydia Becker and the Cause, 1992, Audrey Kelly	£5.95
From Lancaster to the Lakes: the Region in Literature, 1992, eds Keith Hanley and Alison Millbank	£5.95
Walking Roman Roads in Bowland, 1992, Philip Graystone	£5.50
Windermere in the Nineteenth Century, 1991, ed. Oliver M. Westall	£4.95
A Traditional Grocer: T. D. Smith's of Lancaster 1858–1981, 1991, ed. Michael Winstanley	£4.95
The Roman Fort and Town of Lancaster, 1990, David Shotter and Andrew White	£4.95
Grand Fashionable Nights: Kendal Theatre, 1989, Margaret Eddershaw	£3.95
Rural Life in South West Lancashire, 1988, Alistair Mutch	£3.95
The Diary of William Fisher of Barrow, 1986, eds William Rollinson and Brett Harrison	£2.95
Popular Leisure and the Music Hall in 19th-Century Bolton, 1982, Robert Poole	£2.95
Richard Marsden and the Preston Chartists, 1981, J. E. King	£2.95

Each of these titles may be ordered by post from the above address, postage and packing £1.00 per order. Please make cheques payable to 'The University of Lancaster'. Titles are also available from all good booksellers in the region.